BEHAVIOR AND
HANDLING OF SHIPS

BEHAVIOR AND HANDLING OF SHIPS

Henry H. Hooyer

CORNELL MARITIME PRESS
Centreville, Maryland

Library of Congress Cataloging-in-Publication Data

Hooyer, Henry H.
   Behavior and handling of ships.

   Bibliography: p.
   1. Ships—Seakeeping. 1. Ship handling. I. Title.
VM156.H66   1983   623.88   83-71312
ISBN 0-87033-306-2

Manufactured in the United States of America

First edition; third printing, 2004

A ship can be more successfully and safely handled by taking advantage of, and cooperating with, the elements to the fullest extent—instead of disregarding and working against them.
—Carlyle J. Plummer, *Ship Handling in Narrow Channels*

Contents

Contents

Contents

Contents

BEHAVIOR AND HANDLING OF SHIPS

Introduction

Les données sur lesquelles le manoeuvrier se base sont rarement mesurables exactement et doivent être appréciées d'instant en instant.
—Pierre Célérier, *La Manoeuvre des Navires*

When we compare a tanker of 250,000-dwt (deadweight ton) with one of 25,000-dwt, we notice that the horsepower propelling the big ship is not anywhere near ten times the horsepower of the ship that is ten times smaller. In fact, it may be less than three times as much, and yet, the relatively low horsepower can give the VLCC (very large crude carrier) the same speed at sea as the smaller tanker.

Under normal sea conditions the VLCC doesn't compare unfavorably to the supertanker, as the first 25,000 tonner was called in the 1950s. The steering, apart from an apparent response lag, poses no particular problem at sea. It is when we come to the point of taking off speed that we find we need a lot of room. Stopping a loaded 250,000-dwt tanker, going at full speed, may take more than three miles in stopping distance and over twenty minutes in time.

Shiphandling Opportunity

In order to know the possibilities and limitations of the big tankers, one should have an opportunity to try them out without a risk. Such an opportunity does, in fact, ex-

3

ist at the Shiphandling Training Center at Port Revel near Grenoble, France, where a fleet of model tankers in scale one to twenty-five is operated on a lake.

Not only do ship models offer a unique opportunity to handle scale replicas of big tankers under different conditions, but they also offer an instructive overall view of the maneuver in a protracted time. As a consequence of working in scale, there is a lot of shiphandling in this miniature world in a comparatively short time, as the action—in the one to twenty-five scale—is five times faster than in real life.

While I was observing and analyzing the maneuvers on the lake, it became clear to me that the position of the pivot point plays a crucial role in explaining the ship's behavior. When the actual pivot point is taken into account, every movement of the ship can be seen as a logical result of the effect of forces acting on the ship. Scale model and prototype are affected in the same way insofar as forces under control, the natural element water, and the capriciousness of wind-force and wind direction are concerned. There is, of course, the difference in size and time scale, but the outcome of the maneuver is the same, in performance as well as in sensation.

Sidon, Lebanon, offered me an opportunity to come back to the real ships. And, I experienced again the similarity of the real ship to the model as I had before experienced the similarity of the model to the real ship when I came from the busy oil-handling port of Aruba to the Shiphandling Training Center. Although I had never handled a ship in a conventional sea berth, the operation was familiar to me because of practice on the lake at Port Revel.

Berthing tankers of up to 150,000-dwt in a CBM (conventional buoy mooring, also called a multiple buoy mooring) in Sidon is done without tug assistance; the ship-handling depends to a large extent on anchor- and line-handling. The position of the pivot point has to be taken into account when we want to take full advantage of the ship's handling characteristics. I hope that an explanation of the mooring and unmooring procedure, which is dealt with in Chapter 6, will give masters and deck officers a better understanding of the maneuver.

A loan-assignment to Ras Tanura, Saudi Arabia, in 1970, was extended to an eight month's stay in a port that can boast of being the largest oil-shipping port in the world. It gave me an opportunity to study the effect of current on all types of ships from the smallest freighter, coming in for bunkers, to the largest tanker afloat.

In 1974, when I came back to Ras Tanura as a senior harbor pilot, Juaymah opened up, which gave me an opportunity to handle ships up to 477,000-dwt to the monobuoy. My Ras Tanura experience is worked out in Chapter 8, "Practical Applications." Throughout this chapter it can be seen how important it is to have a good idea about the location of the pivot point during dockings and undockings. Mooring and unmooring to a single buoy mooring are dealt with in Chapter 3.

My return to Aruba in 1981 led me to upgrade the water depth and the size of tankers handled in the inner harbor of San Nicolas. During the years I was away from the island, two reef berths had been added where the largest tankers could dock. Here, I had an opportunity to upgrade the size of ships personally handled to well over 500,000-dwt.

Considerations

5

The maneuvers I discuss in the text are examples of maneuvers I have observed again and again either with model tankers or with the real ships, or, in most cases, with both. For handling ships in canals and rivers, there is no better instruction to be found than in *Ship Handling in Narrow Channels* by Carlyle J. Plummer. This book was my guide to "mud piloting"; I refer to it in the paragraph on meeting and passing in Chapter 7.

The numerical values used in the examples, representing current force or windforce, are not accurate and the position of the pivot point is guesswork. Shiphandling is judgment and feel. It is difficult to accurately measure all forces that affect the ship and to calculate their effect on the maneuver. The numerical values in various situations of wind and current serve their purpose inasmuch as they give us an impression of the magnitude of wind- and current force in relation to the magnitude of other forces acting on the ship simultaneously which will help us in explaining the ship's behavior.

All ships considered have single right-handed propellers. In cases where a bow thruster is involved we can consider the effect of the bow thruster as being similar to the effect of a tug at the bow. Attention is given to cases where it does make a difference and where either of the two is preferable.

Variables in Shiphandling

It has been said that no two pilots dock a ship exactly the same way. It can even be said that the same pilot will never dock the same ship the same way twice because there are too many variables involved in shiphandling.

The "Human Factor"

There are time delays between the order and the execution of the order: for instance, when the officer who should be near the telegraph is, for one reason or another, not near the telegraph, or is answering the telephone. In case there is no bridge control we may have another time lag due to response (or lack of it) of the engineer in charge in the engine room. There is the man at the wheel who receives his relayed orders when the man who gives the orders is outside on the bridgewing. The officers and crew fore and aft have different responses depending upon skill, training, etc. Furthermore, the skippers on the assisting tugs are individuals with different responses, capabilities, and skills.

Communications

The communication between bridge and fore- and aft ship can be poor, the telephone may not be easily accessible, walkie-talkies may not be working properly, the talk-back system may not be clearly understandable, winches may be too noisy, etc. In case of different nationalities there can be language problems leading to misunderstandings of orders. Even when people speak the same language they can fail to understand each other because of their inability to express themselves clearly. There can also be misunderstandings through unhappy coincidence.

Mechanical Faults and Failures

Failure or malfunctioning of rudder, engine, bow thruster, or assisting tug happen occasionally. Furthermore, anchors

7

may fail to drop, winches may break down, steam pipes may burst, heaving lines may fall short of docks or may get tangled up, mooring lines or towropes may break, etc.

Forces Not Under Control

Wind and current may change in direction and or force. Shallow water effects are not always predictable. In the case of docking a different ship we have different engine power and engine response, different draft, different trim, different size and momentum, different superstructure, different tugs or skippers, etc. It would indeed be coincidence if two dockings were exactly similar.

However, what all ships—including scale models—have in common in shiphandling is that they move through the water. To better understand ship behavior, we will examine the consequences and effects of the vessel's motion through the water.

Principles of Shiphandling

Motion of the ship has to be perceived through constant observation. The ship can be under longitudinal or lateral motion or both. At the same time the ship can have rotational motion. In most cases we cannot move the ship sideways without having rotational motion as well, except when we have tug assistance.

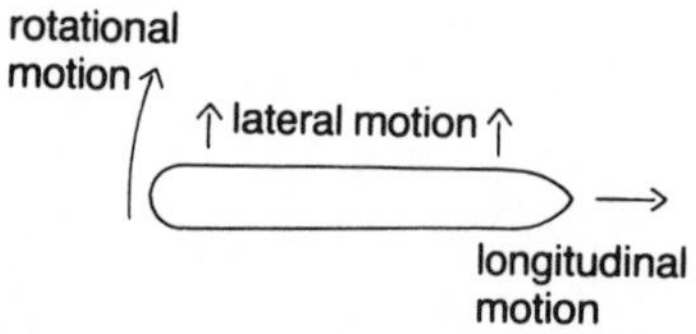

When the ship is under rotational motion we must take into consideration the **pivot point** in order to assess the leverage of the force that causes the ship to rotate. The moment of a force about a point is the product of that force and the perpendicular on its line of action. Thus, it makes a big difference whether the point of impact of a force exerted on the ship is

Fig 1. Components of ship's motion.

close to the pivot point or far away from it. On a big ship the distance from point of impact to pivot point can be hundreds of feet. A shift in the position of the pivot point of a couple of hundred feet greatly affects the moment of the rotational force and consequently the product measured in feet/tons. The farther the point of impact of a force acting on the ship is from the pivot point, the longer the lever of that force and the greater its effective leverage. As the pivot point can shift during the maneuver, it is important to have an idea about the possible position of the pivot point under a different set of conditions to anticipate a change in rotational motion.

Momentum comes into play when we want to slow down or change direction. By definition, momentum is the quantity of motion measured by the product of mass and velocity. Generally, we consider momentum as motion of the ship at the time we no longer want it, especially when we have taken action to obtain the opposite effect. When proceeding at the same speed, a loaded ship carries more momentum than one in light condition, and a big ship carries more momentum than a small one.

Frictional drag has relatively less retarding effect on the bigger ship because the displacement varies with the cube of the ship's dimensions, whereas the wetted area varies with the square of the ship's dimensions. From a position dead in the water, it takes the relatively low horsepower of the big ship a very long time to overcome inertia and bring the ship up to full speed. Once under way, the relatively low horsepower can sustain speed at comparatively low fuel consumption because of the relatively small wetted area and consequently low frictional drag. However, when it comes to the point of stopping the VLCC, the momentum carries on so much longer. The only way to keep the product of mass and velocity down on the VLCC is to keep the speed down.

Momentum has to be anticipated: when we want to stop the ship from going ahead, we deal with longitudinal momentum, and when we want to stop the ship from moving sideways, we deal with lateral momentum. When the ship's momentum acts as a force, we must consider the center of gravity as the point of impact of the force. The effect of momentum, acting as a force, has to be considered with respect to the pivot point. We will see that momentum can start or sustain rotational motion. When we want to stop rotational motion, we must deal with rotational momentum.

Because of the viscosity and low compressibility of water, **resistance** is put up against movement of the ship through the water. There will be a rise in water level in the direction of the ship's motion accompanied by a lowering in water level on the opposite side. At low speed, frictional resistance is responsible for most of the underwater resistance met by the vessel. Frictional resistance depends upon the wetted area and the state of the hull (fouling); it increases with speed and causes frictional wake.

Longitudinal resistance is met when pressure builds up ahead of the ship; energy is absorbed and dissipated by setting up a wave-system at higher speed. Although a bulbous bow offers less resistance, the longitudinal resistance comes up to about the same proportion of the propulsion force at higher speed.

Lateral resistance is met under lateral motion. The magnitude of longitudinal and lateral resistance depends upon the ship's shape and speed through the water, and is directly proportionate to the ship's propulsion force when the ship is at constant speed. Both longitudinal and lateral resistance act as forces and play a role in determining the position of the pivot point.

The shiphandler must judge how much the ship is affected by each of the forces acting on the ship. Not only is it important to assess the magnitude of a force, but the shiphandler must also have an idea about the leverage of that force. For this reason he or she must be aware of each motion of the ship through the water, evaluating constantly the forces affecting the ship and considering how to cope with them in order to maintain a balance of forces.

A force exerted on a ship will result in motion after inertia has been overcome. Once moving through the water, the ship displaces water and meets underwater resistance. That part of the underwater resistance which plays an important role in shiphandling is the resistance force which acts on the opposite side of the hull as the exerted force and in opposite direction to that force.

The propulsion force results in longitudinal motion. Longitudinal resistance exerts a backward force at the bow which opposes forward motion of the ship (Fig. 2, 1). The bow thruster force results in rotational motion; underwater resistance is at the ship's side mostly forward (Fig. 2,2). A beam wind causes the ship to move sideways through the water. Underwater resistance, in this case, lateral resistance, acts in opposite direction to the wind-force (Fig. 2,3). A beam current, on the other hand, causes the ship to go sideways with-

Motion and Resistance

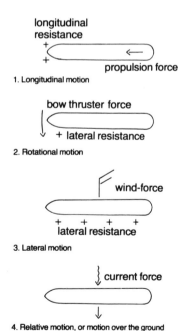

1. Longitudinal motion

2. Rotational motion

3. Lateral motion

4. Relative motion, or motion over the ground

Fig 2. The four motions.

11

out meeting underwater resistance. The lateral motion is, in this case, over the ground (Fig. 2,4). After course alteration, or when the ship gets out of the current, the relative motion manifests itself as momentum.

In shiphandling we may have to deal with all four motions simultaneously.

Judging Motion

In berthing big tankers the aim in shiphandling is, in most cases, to try and obtain a singular lateral motion and prevent rotational motion from developing at the moment of making contact with the dock, not only because it is necessary to spread the area of contact over all mooring dolphins, but also because it is easier to check lateral motion through the water than it is to stop rotational motion.

Rudder and propeller produce a combination of the three motions. It is only when we have full control over forces (tugs) at our disposal that we have full control over forces acting on the ship. By balancing the forces we can eliminate undesirable motion and leave only motion in one direction, or we can stop this motion altogether in time.

It is interesting to compare the resulting rotational motion under the effect of using the rudder with propeller working ahead, the bow thruster, and the propeller working astern (Fig. 3.). From our position on the bridge—aft, midships, or even far forward—we must judge how much of the ship's motion is longitudinal, how much is lateral, and how much is rotational. At the same time we must be able to assess how much motion we need in each direction and be prepared to slow down or stop any of the three motions in time.

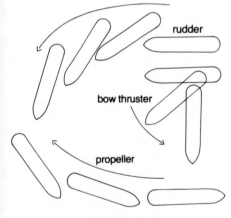

Fig 3. Rotational motion in combination with longitudinal and/or lateral motion.

12

The direction of longitudinal motion of the ship determines to a very large extent the position of the pivot point. The center of rotational motion has to be taken into account in our appraisal of the turning moment; a good appreciation of the location of the pivot point provides the key to a successful maneuver.

Speed of approach can be safely judged visually up to the tonnage of the MST (medium-sized tanker). However, a safe speed of approach of the VLCC and up has reached such a low order that instrument readings have become very helpful—if not essential, especially at night— for docking as well as for anchoring.

Judgment and Instruments

Many large tankers are fitted out with a Doppler instrument, although there is not always a docking Doppler indicator on the bridgewing and, if there is one, it is not always operational. Some of the Doppler instruments indicate whether the speed is through the water (W) or over the ground (G). If this indication is lacking, it is sometimes not clear what the indicated speed represents.

When the Doppler indicator gives only the lateral speed of the foreship—besides the longitudinal speed—we need the information of the rate of turn indicator to deduct the lateral speed aft.

Some terminals have a speed of approach instrument to measure the speed of the incoming ship, information which can be relayed to the ship, or shown either by colored lights or by means of a dial giving the actual speed. A shore Doppler is most useful at the time when the propeller is working astern, and the readings of the ship's Doppler of one knot or less become unreliable.

To assess the **angle of approach** the compass repeater nearby on the bridge-wing is very helpful. Readings from docking Doppler, compass repeater, rudder angle, and engine revolutions should be within easy reach from the far end of the bridgewing. The bridgewing should extend to the the ship's side to enable us to actually see the ship coming in all the way to the moment of touching the mooring dolphins.

Furthermore, quite a few ships have a **wind** speed/direction indicator, information from which is very useful, particularly at night.

Information on **current** from shore-based instruments is seldom available. In case the ship is fitted out with a Doppler sonar which gives speed over the ground as well as speed through the water, the speed of a head current is the difference between the two readings. The readings of the lateral motion over the ground give the speed of the current on the beam when other forces such as wind and side momentum from turning can be neglected. At the time when information from instrument readings is not critical, the readings may serve us to adjust our judgment by comparison.

Approximations of Magnitude of Forces

We will identify the forces acting on the ship and examine their effect under different conditions. When the pivot point is taken into account, every movement of the ship can be seen as caused by forces acting on the ship; seemingly "irrational" behavior of the ship can be explained, predicted, and anticipated.

In order to explain the behavior of the ship we will use approximate equivalent values of some of the forces under consideration. For example:

$$100 \text{ HP } = 1 \text{ ton bollard pull}$$

$$\text{longitudinal resistance } = 25 \text{ percent of propulsion force under constant speed}$$

transverse force of propeller
working astern = 5 to 10 percent of applied stern power

These figures are only approximations. They will serve us by giving an impression of the magnitude of these forces in relation to the magnitude of other forces acting on the ship simultaneously. The magnitude of the other forces will be dealt with in the relevant chapters.

During the maneuver there is very little time for calculations. Moreover, the forces are difficult to measure under changing conditions. The shiphandler constantly observes and appraises the ship's motion as well as the forces acting on the ship, and, because of his experience, he can anticipate the ship's next move without mathematics.

CHAPTER ONE

The Peripatetic Pivot Point

*There may be more than a dozen forces act-
ing about the vessel's axes at a given moment,
and the resultant may not be as anticipated
but due partially to a force which has
escaped discovery. This is not "mysticism"
as much as lack of the research which takes
the art of shiphandling into the finite world
of applied science.*
　　　　　—P. F. Willerton, *Basic Shiphandling*

The motion of a turning ship can be seen
as a combination of longitudinal, lateral,
and rotational motion of which both longitudinal and lateral motion can be zero.
The rotational motion itself is about a
vertical axis. The position of this axis on
the ship is influenced by the ship's shape,
the ship's motion, the magnitude, and
point of impact of the various forces acting
on the ship. As the axis moves about with
a change of the ship's motion and with a
change in the forces that affect the ship,
we can speak of a mobile axis. If this
vertical axis were visible we would see
the top of it from above as a spot; this
point we call the pivot point.

　In the following paragraphs we will
examine the effect of change in motion of
the ship on the pivot point and the effect
of various forces acting on the ship with
respect to the pivot point. We will see that
we cannot speak of "the" pivot point as a
fixed point, but that the pivot point wan-
ders about and is, in fact, a peripatetic
pivot point.

16

The reason the pivot point is hard to place in shiphandling theory is probably due to the dual nature of the effect of underwater resistance. The major part of this resistance is made up of frictional drag and, as it takes place all along the hull, it has no effect on the position of the pivot point. Thus, we do not have to take it into account.

Let us assume that the propulsion force has overcome frictional drag. In figure 4, the remainder of the propulsion force (roughly one quarter) is represented by a vector acting at the center of gravity G. At the bow, opposing the ship's progress, is a vector representing the longitudinal resistance (about one quarter of the total underwater resistance). At constant speed the two vectors are of equal length, because otherwise the ship would accelerate/decelerate.

When the turn sets in under the effect of rudder, the initial pivot point will be between the bow and G. The position of G is indicated by the trim, and only when the ship is on an even keel is the position of G at middle length and the initial pivot point at one quarter length.

The ratio of longitudinal resistance to propulsion force (res/prop ratio) plays an important role in establishing the position of the pivot point. The direction of the propulsion force is the same as the ship's heading, whereas the direction of the momentum lags, tending to continue in the original direction of motion.

Under the turn (fig. 5), the underwater pressure will spread from the bow along the ship's side. With a widening of the drift angle, the ship's side will be more exposed and the increase in pressure will cause a loss of speed. The pressure forward of the pivot point tends to push the

Position of Pivot Point

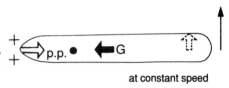

at constant speed

Fig. 4. Initial pivot point.

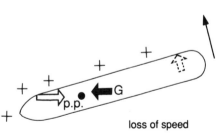

loss of speed

Fig. 5. The pivot point under the turn.

17

pivot point closer to midships, while the pressure abaft the pivot point, by acting against the turn, limits the drift angle. On a directionally stable ship, the turn will eventually stop after the rudder has been put amidships.

A rotational motion may be the result of several forces acting on the ship simultaneously. The position of the pivot point then depends upon the magnitude and point of impact of the several forces acting on the ship. Since the pivot point is liable to shift with a change in magnitude or with a shift in point of impact of one of the forces acting on the ship, the several forces have a varying degree of leverage, depending upon the position of the pivot point.

Longitudinal Motion and Pivot Point

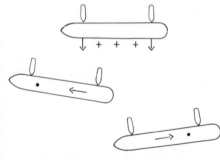

Fig. 6. Tugs push with equal force equidistant from midships.

We consider a loaded tanker, on even keel, assisted by two tugs of equal power, one forward and one aft (fig. 6). The tugs are pushing with equal force at equal distance from amidships. As long as the ship develops no headway or sternway, the result of the tugs' effort is sheer lateral motion of the ship. However, as soon as the ship starts moving through the water, ahead or astern, we see that a swing develops.

Forward motion of the ship brings the center of lateral resistance forward. The forward tug is pushing against greater opposition than the after tug, which makes the forward tug have less net lateral effect. The imbalance in forces results in rotational motion. The position of the pivot point depends upon the ship's motion through the water and the relative strength of the tugs.

We can simply say that head motion brings the pivot point forward which shortens the distance of the point of impact of the forward tug to the pivot point and con-

18

sequently reduces the effective leverage of the forward tug. At the same time, the distance of the point of impact of the after tug to the pivot point increases, which in turn increases the effective leverage of the after tug.

Stern motion brings the pivot point aft, which reverses the rotational effect of the transverse forces exerted on the ship by the tugs.

When the tugs push with equal power at equal distance from amidships we see that longitudinal motion of the ship results in rotational motion as a side effect of the transverse forces exerted by the tugs. Conversely, when a swing sets in while the tugs push with equal power, we can conclude that the ship must be under longitudinal motion through the water.

If no swing is required we can either slow down the tug that causes the rotational effect or we can stop the longitudinal motion of the ship through the water. Reversing the longitudinal motion will result in an eventual reversal of the rotational motion (see Appendix A).

The leverage of other transverse forces that are beam wind, bow thruster, rudder, etc., will be similarly affected by longitudinal motion of the ship.

Wind Effect and Pivot Point

Let us consider a light ship, dead in the water, affected by a beam wind (fig. 7a). The wind causes the ship to drift to leeward, and the hull meets underwater resistance. As the ship is down by the stern, more resistance is met by the underwater after part of the ship. The result is that the center of lateral resistance R will be abaft midships.

On a light ship, with the bow high out of the water, the forward part of the ship

19

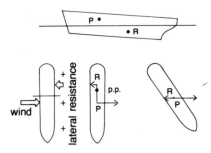

Fig. 7a. Wind effect on ballasted ship, dead in the water.

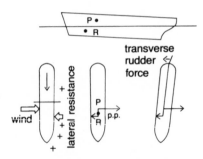

Fig. 7b. Wind effect on ship under headway.

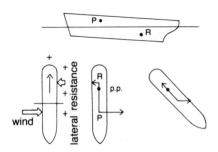

Fig.7c. Wind effect on ship under sternway.

will be more affected by the wind than the after part. The wind pressure can be represented by a vector which is the wind-force acting on the center of pressure P. The underwater resistance can be represented by a vector which is the force of the underwater resistance at R. As long as P is not vertically above R, the two forces turn the ship, and the ensuing pivot point will be between P and R.

In the case of wind effect on a ship under headway, the center of lateral resistance will move forward, and—specifically on vessels with the bridge aft—the center of pressure P will be abaft the center of underwater resistance R (fig. 7b). With the pivot point forward, the transverse wind-force cants the ship so that the ship's heading makes an angle with the intended course. To control this angle and counterbalance the wind-force we need a transverse force aft—the rudder. A swing develops when there is an imbalance in transverse forces.

Stern motion takes the center of lateral resistance aft which increases the leverage of the transverse wind-force (fig. 7c). The rudder force has no effective leverage while the ship is backing. Since the propeller wash is no longer directed against the rudder face, the rudder meets resistance of the water only, resulting in a small transverse rudder force.

The ship is bodily blown to leeward, the bow faster than the stern, so that under sternway the stern moves up into the wind, or is "seeking the wind." However, the stern will only go up into the wind when the bow has room to drift and is allowed to fall off. The pivot point moves far aft, providing more leverage to the wind-force.

The transverse thrust of a right-handed propeller, working astern, is easily overcome by a strong wind on the starboard bow.

The rudder induces a transverse force at the after end of the ship when the rudder is put over on a ship under headway. Underwater resistance starts developing a transverse force on the exposed bow as soon as the swing sets in. The resultant lateral resistance forward acts in opposite direction to the transverse component of the rudder force (fig. 8).

First we will consider the effect of the propulsion force and the rudder on a ship that starts from dead in the water. Inertia causes the ship to resist acceleration. Underwater resistance plays, as yet, no significant role. The longitudinal propulsion force is concurrently working to overcome longitudinal inertia and lateral (rotational) inertia when part of this force is converted into transverse rudder force. The rudder force, exerted at the very end of the ship, overcomes lateral inertia of the vessel sooner than the propulsion force overcomes longitudinal inertia because of its leverage. The center of the ensuing rotational motion depends on the L/B (length to beam) ratio of the vessel. A ship with an L/B ratio of 8, for instance, starting with zero longitudinal speed through the water, has the initial pivot point at ⅛ L from the bow. The rudder force works at an optimum when the ship is dead in the water, and full thrust on the rudder has maximal leverage.

After longitudinal inertia has been overcome and the ship gathers headway, underwater resistance builds up. The under-

Rudder Effect and Pivot Point

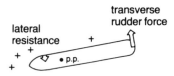

Fig. 8. Lateral resistance and rudder force.

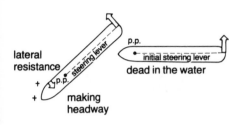

Fig. 9. Decrease in rudder leverage caused by headway.

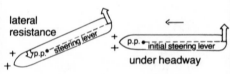

Fig. 10. Decrease in rudder leverage under prolonged rudder while under headway.

water resistance reaches a magnitude of about one quarter of the propulsion force, causing the pivot point to move away from the forward position proportionately to the magnitude of this force in relation to the propulsion force (fig. 9). Thus the distance of the pivot point to the stern is reduced by $\frac{1}{4}$ of the initial distance, leaving a steering lever of $\frac{3}{4} \times \frac{7}{8}$ L = $\frac{21}{32}$ L. The distance from the pivot point to the bow is then $\frac{11}{32}$ L (where L is the length between perpendiculars). The pivot point stays in the same position when the ship is turning at a constant speed.

When a ship is proceeding on a straight course there should, ideally, be no lateral resistance. Rudder effect resulting in course alteration will have an initial pivot point located at a distance from the bow proportionate to the res/prop ratio (ratio of longitudinal resistance to propulsion force), that is, about $\frac{1}{4}$ L from forward (fig. 10). The underwater resistance which was acting on the bow under longitudinal motion will, during the turn, also affect the laterally exposed ship's side. The lateral resistance on the exposed bow pushes the pivot point back and consequently shortens the steering lever. The reduction in steering lever is proportionate to the L/B ratio. For a ship with an L/B ratio of 8, for instance, turning at a constant speed, the reduced steering lever will be about $\frac{7}{8} \times \frac{3}{4}$ L = $\frac{21}{32}$ L, which again leaves the distance from bow to pivot point at $\frac{11}{32}$ L.

It is generally assumed that the pivot point on a ship, under headway and turning under rudder, lies at about one third of the length from forward. This is not far from the theoretical position. For L/B ratios of 9, 8, 7, 6, and 5 we find respectively: $\frac{1}{3}$ L, $\frac{21}{32}$ L, $\frac{5}{14}$ L, $\frac{3}{8}$ L and $\frac{2}{5}$ L

22

from forward. However, the actual position of the pivot point is not only determined by such factors as L/B ratio and state of the hull, but also trim has a very strong effect on it and under acceleration and deceleration of the ship the pivot point moves temporarily more forward or aft.

Rotational Inertia and Pivot Point

From a position dead in the water with full ahead on the engine on full rudder, it is easier to overcome rotational inertia than longitudinal inertia. For one thing, while longitudinal inertia prevents the ship from going ahead, the transverse rudder force has maximal leverage.

Motor ships have the advantage of an immediate powerful thrust on the rudder, which translates directly into transverse rudder force. The strong impetus of the transverse rudder force overcomes rotational inertia before longitudinal motion sets in, causing the ship to turn on the spot. It is longitudinal inertia that helps us make a tight swing.

Turbine-powered ships build up engine revolutions so slowly that more time is allowed for longitudinal inertia to be overcome before rotational motion is well under way. The ship starts creeping ahead while the swing sets in very slowly, reducing, as it does, the rudder leverage.

Rotational Momentum and Pivot Point

The pivot point is the center of a rotational motion. This rotational motion results in rotational momentum, the magnitude of which depends upon the mass of the ship. Once a rotational momentum has developed, the influence of a newly introduced force acting on the ship does not have an immediate effect on

23

the position of the pivot point, and the leverage of this new force depends for a while upon the existing pivot point. When the point of impact of this force is close to the pivot point, the new force has little rotational effect. With loss of rotational momentum, the pivot point will gradually move to a position commensurate to the magnitude and point of impact of this new force. The new force will grow in rotational effect with the increase of effective leverage.

A good example is a loaded tanker moving astern through the water with the bow swinging to starboard. To stop the swing we give full ahead on hard left rudder. Although we can see the propeller wash we notice very little effect of the rudder force. It takes quite a long time before we see the swing reverse; the rudder force simply doesn't have enough leverage as long as the pivot point is aft. When sternway comes off, the rudder starts having a better effect.

Propeller Effect and Pivot Point

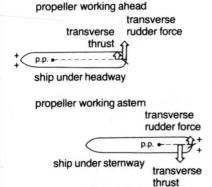

Fig. 11. Transverse rudder force and transverse thrust.

The thrust of the upper blades against the rudder may produce a somewhat greater transverse force than the thrust of the lower blades, or the lower blades encounter more resistance; the latter is apparent when the propeller is only partially submerged. In any case, the resulting side force from a fully submerged propeller working ahead is a small transverse force which pushes the stern to starboard (fig. 11). The maximum effect is on a ship starting from dead in the water, when the initial pivot point is far forward and the transverse thrust has maximal leverage.

Under head motion the effect is easily offset by negligible corrective rudder. On the full turning circle, however, it can be

24

noticed that a full turn to port is usually smaller than a full turn to starboard, especially on ships with relatively big propellers.

The propeller working astern produces a strong transverse thrust because the helical discharge is directed against the stern where it hits the hull, in part, almost at right angles (fig. 12). Large-diameter propellers of low-speed revolution push back a greater amount of water under a steeper angle against the stern and produce a strong transverse thrust on working astern. A propeller duct, on the other hand, prevents the water from reaching the stern under a steep angle, thus producing less transverse thrust when the engine is working astern on a ship fitted out with a shrouded propeller.

The effect of the transverse thrust of the propeller working astern is greatest when the pivot point is forward, that is, when the ship is still under forward motion or stopped in the water. The transverse thrust loses out in leverage when the pivot point moves aft.

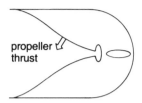

Fig. 12. Right-handed propeller working astern.

Sternway and Pivot Point

The position of the pivot point on a ship under sternway depends upon the trim, the speed of the ship through the water, the leverage of the transverse force which causes the ship to rotate, and the influence of the other forces acting on the ship simultaneously.

The effect of trim is reversed under sternway, that is, a good trim for steering under headway turns into the characteristics of a trim by the head under sternway. The pivot point, which was far forward under headway, will, under reversed longitudinal motion through

25

the water, move to a position not so far aft because of trim condition.

The position of the pivot point under sternway is affected by the propeller wash, which is directed against the stern. While the propeller is working astern (fig. 11), the combined forces of transverse thrust and increased directional resistance tend to keep the pivot point away from a position farther aft where it would otherwise settle with the propeller stopped. It can be seen, for instance, in figure 65, where the engine is working astern, that the pivot point has not moved so far aft as in figure 71, where the engine has been stopped.

After stopping the engine on a backing ship, we notice an increase in rotational effect of a wind on the beam when a shift farther aft of the pivot point results in a gain of leverage for the transverse wind-force.

The transverse force of bow thruster, or tug on the bow, on a ship under sternway easily overcomes—and turns the ship against—the transverse thrust of the propeller. Under the ensuing rotational motion against the direction of the transverse thrust, the pivot point tends to shift farther aft, thus reducing the leverage of the transverse thrust of the propeller (App. B, 5E).

Note: The dockings and undockings discussed in the text take place alongside piers built on a pile structure. Because of the open face under this type of jetty, there is no effect of propeller wash between ship and dock when the engine is working astern.

CHAPTER TWO

Rudder and Propeller

The art of shiphandling involves the effective use of forces under control to overcome the effect of forces not under control.
　　—Charles H. Cotter, *The Master and His Ship*

By deflecting the propeller thrust—on a single-screw ship, right-handed propeller, engine working ahead—the rudder exerts a force at the after end of the ship. This force can be resolved into a transverse force and a longitudinal force. It is the transverse force that we need for steering the ship; the longitudinal force, which causes a reduction in speed, is a loss from a navigational point of view, but it may be the very thing we need when making the approach to a berth.

In case we want to slow down without working the engine astern, we can deliberately use full rudder as much as possible.

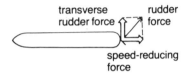

Fig. 13. Rudder effect.

In order to find out how a ship under headway is affected by the transverse rudder force, we consider its effect on the center of gravity with respect to the pivot point. As the transverse rudder force lifts the center of gravity, the pivot point can be seen to function as a fulcrum and the center of gravity as the weight to be lifted (Appendix B, 1). After inertia has been overcome, the center of gravity moves into a sidewise direction and the opening of

Rudder Force, Drift Angle, and Lateral Resistance

27

the drift angle causes the ship's side to meet underwater resistance. The position of the pivot point plays a pivotal role in proportioning the lateral resistance.

The effect of the lateral resistance forward of the pivot point is twofold: it assists the swing because it has the same rotational direction as the transverse rudder force; and, concomitantly, it pushes the pivot point back, thereby shortening the steering lever (fig. 14). With the introduction of lateral resistance the turning moment is made up of the steering moment and the moment of lateral resistance (Appendix B, 2).

The lateral resistance abaft the pivot point restricts the drift angle and consequently limits the magnitude of the lateral resistance. The drift angle opens up to the point where the lateral resistance abaft the pivot point comes up to a certain proportion of the transverse rudder force complementary to the frictional resistance.

A narrow ship has a relatively longer underwater area abaft the pivot point and meets relatively greater lateral resistance aft, resulting in a smaller drift angle and consequently wider turn (fig. 15). A beamy ship meets relatively greater underwater resistance forward of the pivot point and less lateral resistance abaft the pivot point, resulting in a wider drift angle and consequently a relatively shorter turn (Appendix B, 3).

Lateral resistance causes loss of speed proportionate to the drift angle and to the increase of exposed underwater area. When the swing has set in and the speed is coming down, lateral resistance and rudder force preserve a competitive balance by means of minimal changes in both drift angle and in position of pivot point.

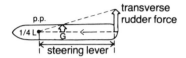

Fig. 14. Effect of transverse rudder force on a ship under speed: initial steering lever.

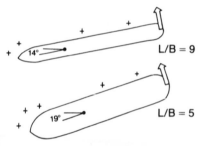

Fig. 15. Effect of beam on pivot point and drift angle.

When we put the rudder back to mid-ships, we notice that the ship continues to swing to port: in addition to the rotational momentum there is a turning moment generated by the ship's lateral momentum and the lateral resistance forward of the pivot point (fig. 16). Lateral momentum acts as a force with the center of gravity as point of impact. The point of impact of the lateral resistance is about halfway between the bow and the pivot point.

In order to stop the swing we put on counter rudder, in our case: full right rudder (fig. 17). The reason it takes more time and more rudder to straighten up than to start a swing is that the lateral resistance remains acting for a while on the opposite bow, working in opposite rotational direction to the rudder (see also Appendix B, 5E).

If we put the rudder back to midships at the moment the swing stops under counter rudder, the swing to port will resume because we break up the balance of forces that exists between transverse rudder force, lateral momentum, and lateral resistance. As long as lateral momentum is on, there is lateral resistance; the two forces form a turning couple which regenerates the swing if unchecked by the rudder. As the lateral momentum decreases gradually, we take off counter rudder accordingly to keep the ship steady.

Acceleration and deceleration play a role in positioning the pivot point when engine revolutions are increased or decreased. Let us consider, for instance, a 50,000-dwt tanker, diesel, proceeding on dead slow, 40 RPM, making a speed of 5.7 knots. When we increase engine revolutions to 65 RPM,

Lateral Momentum

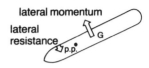

Fig. 16. Lateral momentum and pivot point.

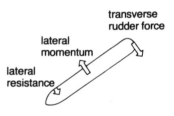

Fig. 17. Steady under counter rudder.

Effect of Longitudinal Inertia on Steering

it takes time before the ship will proceed at the speed of 9.3 knots as indicated on the information sheet for 65 RPM. It is longitudinal inertia which is responsible for the time it takes to come up to the higher speed through the water. During this time lapse, the resistance forward on the ship is not yet proportionate to the increased propulsion force, resulting in a forwarding of the pivot point.

When the ship is under rudder at the moment of increase in engine revs, we have an increased thrust on the rudder as well as a momentarily increased leverage of the rudder while the ship proceeds at a comparatively low speed through the water. The improved steering will last until the resistance forward corresponds again with the engine revs.

The ship will not come up to the indicated speed on the information sheet when the rudder is kept over because part of the propulsion force is diverted into transverse rudder force; and, moreover, the ship is meeting more underwater resistance while turning.

If, for any reason, we cannot afford an increase in speed, but we need a momentary increase in rate of turn, we better take off the extra engine revolutions as soon as possible instead of taking off the rudder. This becomes necessary because, at the time the rudder comes back to midships, all propeller thrust will become available to overcome longitudinal inertia. If left on long enough to increase the ship's speed through the water, we have a relatively higher resistance at the bow when we reduce engine revolutions, resulting in reduced steering leverage.

Effect of Trim on Steering

When moving sideways through the water, the ship down by the head has relatively more of the underwater area forward of the pivot point, which will meet more lateral resistance. A stronger transverse force on the foreship pushes the pivot point farther back and shortens the steering lever. Moreover, the propeller is not so deeply submerged when the ship is light and down by the head, resulting in less thrust on the rudder which, in turn, diminishes the steering moment.

When a swing is on, there is a larger rotational momentum of the foreship which has to be met by a smaller steering moment. The more the ship is down by the head, the more difficult it is to steer the ship. It takes time to start a swing, and it takes even more time to stop the swing. The strong lateral resistance force on the foreship contributes to a small turning circle (Appendix B, 4).

A ship down by the stern has relatively more of the underwater area abaft the pivot point. The foreship meets less underwater resistance when the ship is moving ahead and sideways through the water under full rudder; the pivot point will consequently remain farther forward, which makes for a relatively longer steering lever. Also, the propeller is deeper down in the water and gives a better thrust on the rudder, which increases the rudder force and the steering moment.

The larger turning circle of a ship down by the stern is due to a lessened effect of a weaker lateral resistance force at the bow and a stronger lateral resistance abaft the pivot point which restricts the drift angle (Appendix B, 5).

**Speed Reduction of
Rudder and Propeller**

At sea, rudder angles of less than 20 degrees are preferable, giving good steering effect and relatively little speed reduction. However, when we do want to reduce speed, we can use the speed-reducing effect of the rudder to advantage by alternately giving full rudder to one side and then the other, called rudder cycling. Depending on how much room we have and how far we can allow the ship to veer from the course, we can leave full rudder on for longer or shorter periods. By exposing the ship's sides we take advantage of the lateral resistance as well. Very large tankers, having an extensive underwater body, suffer a considerable loss of speed when turning under full speed, relatively more than the smaller tankers.

On a 477,000-dwt tanker, making 14.4 knots, it took 62 minutes, after stopping the engine, for the speed to come down to 5 knots (inertia test). It took only 5.5 minutes for a similar speed reduction from 14.4 to 5 knots, when turning under full rudder (35 degrees) through 150 degrees, maintaining full speed on the engine! The ship was in loaded condition in both cases, drawing 92 feet and having a rudder area ratio at this draft of 1/60. The rudder area ratio is the relation between wetted rudder area and lateral underwater area of the ship. The same 477,000-dwt tanker in ballast, with a rudder area ratio of 1/27, not only carries less momentum, but also has relatively more rudder. These two factors make rudder cycling with small course alterations more effective in ballast than in loaded condition.

For a speed reduction by propeller, it is noteworthy that on a ship moving at full speed, a propeller working at 20 percent of its capacity meets more resistance of the water than does a stopped propeller.

Dead slow ahead on the engine, after the ship has been on full speed ahead, gives initially a somewhat better braking effect than stopping the propeller immediately altogether.

For a quicker stop from full speed ahead, the propeller working astern at 20 percent of its capacity is initially more effective than working full speed astern, when most of its effect gets lost due to cavitation.

Turning Circles

A complete turn under full rudder and full speed on the engine, starting from dead in the water, takes less than half the room it takes to turn the ship starting from full speed through the water. Turning initially on the spot, the ship gathers headway and, while gaining momentum, the swing grows progressively wider. It is inertia that enables the ship to make a short turn from dead in the water and to resist longitudinal acceleration.

Starting from full speed through the water, the ship ends up turning the full circle inside of the starting point under considerably reduced speed.

Example

A 477,000-dwt tanker, turbine, L/B ratio 6, fully loaded, 92 feet draft; rudder angle 35 degrees; initial speed 14.4 knots, final speed 3 knots. Full speed on the engine: initial RPM, 89, final RPM 78. Time taken for full circle: 16.5 minutes.

After the rudder has been put hard over, the ship starts turning slowly, and it is only after the ship has swung through about 10 degrees that the turning motion picks up. The rate of turn peaks between 10 and 90 degrees and settles at a lower rate when the ship proceeds at a constant speed (Appendix B, 1).

33

Theoretically, the diameter of the turning circle is between 4 L and 3 L (length between perpendiculars) for L/B ratio 9 and 5 respectively (Appendix B, 3). However, much depends upon a number of factors affecting the drift angle, such as trim and bottom clearance.

The turning circle on a constant higher speed is somewhat larger than on a constant lower speed because of the greater momentum, a relatively longer steering lever, and consequently smaller drift angle.

Example

A 50,000-dwt turbine tanker with an L/B ratio of 8; draft: in loaded condition 41 ft 8 ins, even keel: in ballast 20 ft fwd and 24 ft aft.

RPM	80		60		35		20	
Draft	Ld	Ball	Ld	Ball	Ld	Ball	Ld	Ball
Loss in RPM	6	5	4	3	1	2	–	–
Tactical diameter in ship lengths	4	3.85	3.75	3.77	3.55	3.44	3.15	3.10
Time to complete circle in minutes–seconds	12–00	6–40	15–15	8–35	23–00	12–15	42–00	20–30

For comparison, the 477,000-dwt tanker in ballast, draft 33.5 feet forward and 40 feet aft; time taken for full turn on full speed: 14 minutes (initial RPM 91, final RPM 82). Time taken for full turn on half speed: 22 min. (RPM 51 throughout), diameter turning circle about 6 percent smaller.

The turning circle in loaded condition tends to be larger than in ballast. The reason is that the loaded ship has a relatively smaller rudder area ratio as well as a greater momentum and, above all, generally, less bottom clearance. In deep water though, there is not much difference in the turning circles because trim brings most of the loaded tankers on about even keel, resulting in a strong lateral resistance forward.

Restricted bottom clearance in shallow water impedes the flow of water underneath the ship, causing a restricted lateral motion of the aftship. The less bottom clearance, the greater the buildup of water on the side the stern moves toward and the lower the water level on the side the ship moves away from, leading to a smaller drift angle and consequently a wider turn in shallow water.

Wind effect transforms the turning circle. Turning the bow into the wind, under normal trim, and the stern away from the wind, the ship turns faster. Turning the bow away from the wind and pushing the stern up against the wind, the ship turns slower, particularly when the superstructure aft is high, and the engine power relatively poor.

Sea and swell have an adverse effect on the swing. When the ship turns the bow into the swell, lateral resistance, under flat sea condition assisting the swing, is working on the weather bow against the swing (Appendix B, 5E). When the ship turns away from sea and swell, the stern must be pushed up against it.

Not until the speed is constant and the ship free from outside forces, is the turning circle described by the ship as it moves through the water, a real circle as per definition.

Rudder Force and Transverse Thrust

The rudder force plays an insignificant role when the ship is under sternway. Since the ship is seldom under considerable sternway, the force produced by un-

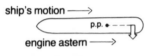

engine astern ⟶

magnitude transverse thrust initially averages about 5 percent of applied stern power

ship's motion ⟶

p.p. •– – –

engine astern ⟶

magnitude transverse thrust under sternway averages about 10 percent of applied stern power

Fig. 18. Transverse thrust and pivot point.

derwater resistance against the rudder face, met during sternway, is small. Moreover, as the pivot point is aft during sternway, the rudder force has little leverage.

A stronger force than the rudder force on a ship going astern is the transverse thrust of the propeller working astern. When the ship is still under forward motion through the water and the engine is working astern, not all of the propeller wash reaches the stern. However, the resulting force has a long lever while the pivot point is still forward. We will put the magnitude of the transverse thrust, while the ship is still moving ahead through the water, at an average of 5 percent of the applied stern power. As head motion comes off, the percentage grows to an average of about 10 percent of the applied stern power when stern motion sets in (fig. 18). However, when the center of lateral resistance moves aft and settles close to the point of impact of the transverse thrust, there is no longer much rotational effect.

When we do not want a ship with a right-handed propeller to swing to starboard, we give a kick ahead on full left rudder before coming astern on the engine. Once sternway has set in, the transverse thrust has little rotational effect. On the other hand, if we do want the ship to turn to the right, we give a kick ahead on full right rudder before coming astern on the engine. By doing so, we have already started rotational motion and introduced a pivot point forward. Longitudinal inertia initially holds the ship back from developing sternway, while maximum transverse thrust has optimal leverage.

Motor ships, having more stern power and consequently stronger transverse thrust as well as quicker engine response

than turbine ships, are easier to turn short
around over starboard. The transverse
thrust is stronger on ships with large and
slow turning propellers than on ships
with small and fast turning propellers.

Rudder Angle

Increasing engine revolutions for better
steering gives only temporarily improved
steering effect and leaves us with an increased ship's speed. Hence in cases where
we cannot afford to have much speed, we
do better not to increase engine revolution
on, for instance, twenty degrees of rudder,
but to use full rudder first of all.

Under sternway, when the propeller
has been stopped, there is some rotational
effect of full rudder. However, since both
the magnitude and the lever of the rudder
force are small, the effect can easily be
nullified by a slight breeze on the opposite
bow.

As long as the ship is moving ahead
through the water, even with the engine
working full astern, we do best to leave the
rudder to that side that we want the ship
to turn to. Not until the ship starts moving astern through the water does it make
sense to put the rudder over to the other
side (the pilot is often reminded that the
rudder is still over while the ship is moving ahead and the engine working astern).

As full rudder partially blocks the inflow of water into the propeller on one
side when the ship is under sternway,
there is a loss of efficiency of the propeller.
A rudder angle of 15 to 20 degrees assures
a better inflow of water as compared to
hard over rudder. We must keep in mind
that the ship is basically designed and
built to go ahead; engine, hull, and propeller design are based on forward motion in

the first place. Is it worthwhile to impair the already poor backing performance of most tankers for what is an academic and, at best, marginal gain in steering? Anyway, since some masters seem reluctant to give full rudder, the pilot can, in this case, keep the master happy by using only 20 degrees of rudder.

CHAPTER THREE

Wind

*Wind is the most powerful conditioning agent
in the whole process of manoeuvering ships.
If it is strong, it exercises a considerable influence on the steering and screw effects of
ships under headway and knocks all common
rules of astern evolutions into a cocked hat.*
—R.A.B. Ardley, *Harbour Pilotage*

The effect of wind depends not only upon
the magnitude of the wind-force, but there
are a number of other factors to be taken
into account when dealing with wind in
shiphandling. Among these factors the
ratio draft/freeboard is very important: a
tanker in ballast may not only have twice
the windage in above-water area, but
there is also less grip on the water because
of light draft. Another important factor is
the angle between the ship's heading and
wind direction. Furthermore, windage increases with increase in deadweight. The
placement of the superstructure and the
change in trim play a role in windage and
rotational effect. Longitudinal motion of
the ship affects the relative distance between the center of pressure and the pivot
point and consequently plays a role in determining the leverage of the transverse
wind-force.

Magnitude of Wind-force

The wind-force can be calculated with the
formula:

wind-force $= 0.004 \times W \times v^2$

where: W = windage in square feet

v = wind speed in knots

wind-force is expressed in pounds

Wind speed as well as wind direction, ship's speed, and ship's heading are not at all times constant during the maneuver. A slight error in wind speed is of much greater consequence than a similar error in assumed windage of the tanker. The following approximations for assumed windage will therefore be good enough for our purpose.

$$W \text{ (abeam)} = LOA \times D - LBP \times \text{mean draft}$$
$$W \text{ (on the bow)} = B \times D - B \times \text{draft forward}$$

where: LOA = length overall
LBP = length between
 perpendiculars
B = breadth, molded
D = depth, molded

For intermediate angles we take the median between the direct proportional value and the value proportional to the sine of the angle of incidence.

On the following pages we will examine the effect of a 25-knot wind on a 70,000-dwt tanker in ballast; draft 16 feet forward and 26 feet aft; LOA = 800 feet; LBP = 765 feet; B = 115 feet; D = 56 ft; engine power = 20,000 HP; and stern power = 16,000 HP.

Head Wind

A wind-force of 25 knots exerts a longitudinal force of about 6 tons on a tanker of 70,000 dwt in ballast. A long as the ship is heading right into the wind, there is no transverse component of the wind-force. When the ship is moving ahead through the water, we have good steering control with the pivot point forward.

Under sternway, the ship is in an unstable equilibrium with the pivot point aft. If a transverse wind-force develops, a long distance to the pivot point and consequently much leverage is created. Since the rudder has very little effect under sternway,

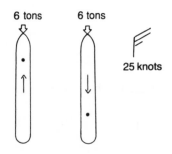

6 tons   6 tons

25 knots

Fig. 19. Effect of head wind on 70,000-dwt tanker in ballast.

we depend on a forward tug or on a bow thruster to keep the ship under control.

With the wind on the bow, there will be an increasing transverse wind-force when the bow falls off. The transverse wind-force grows to about 15 tons when the 25-knot wind is 30 degrees on the port bow and increases to about 27 tons when the ship is heading 60 degrees off the wind. The longitudinal wind-force decreases to about 4 tons with the wind 30 degrees on the bow and to about 2 tons with the wind 60 degrees on the bow.

When moving ahead through the water, the ship will have a tendency to swing to port. Under sternway, there will be a strong tendency for the bow to fall off to starboard; it is only by coming ahead on the engine and bringing the pivot point forward that we can check the swing.

Wind on the Bow

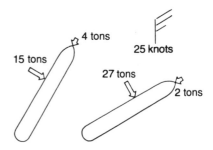

Fig. 20. Effect of wind on the bow.

On the beam, the transverse wind-force of 25 knots exerts a force of 36 tons. The point of impact is forward of the midship because of the trim. Whether or not the tugs can keep the ship under control depends on the horsepower of the tugs and the side on which they are made fast.

Suppose that the ship is assisted by two tugs of 2,000 HP each, one tug forward, one aft. The bollard pull of the tugs is about 35 tons, but in backing they pull only about 13 tons. When the tugs are made fast on the starboard side, the combined force of the tugs can move the ship up against the wind. Backing on the port side, the tugs cannot hold the ship.

With the tugs on the port side, we need at least a strong tug forward. A tug of 4,000 HP, for instance, having a bollard

Beam Wind

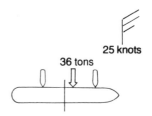

Fig. 21. Effect of wind on the beam.

41

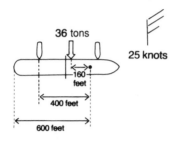

Fig. 22. Beam wind on ship moving ahead through the water.

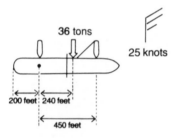

Fig. 23. Beam wind on ship moving astern through the water.

pull of 65 tons and 29 tons on backing, could, in combination with the 2,000 HP tug aft, hold the ship, provided we prevent excessive dynamic loads on the tug's headlines.

When the assisted ship is dead in the water and we have balanced the forces of wind and tugs, we have created a more or less static situation where the forward tug takes more of the load than the after tug.

Under forward motion (fig. 22), we have the rudder with sufficient leverage to correct any imbalance in forces. Let us assume that the point of impact of the windforce is 40 feet forward of the midship and that the forward tug is made fast forward on the main deck, 150 feet from the stem; the after tug, aft on the main deck, 200 feet from the stern. Let us further assume that the pivot point under forward motion is about 200 feet from the stem, providing the rudder with a lever of 600 feet. As long as the forward tug can keep position, we can keep the ship under control.

Under stern motion (fig. 23), with the pivot point aft, 200 feet from the stern, we put a very heavy load on the forward tug. The rotational moment of the beam wind is then 8,640 feet/tons, which requires about a 20-ton pull of the forward tug to check, as the tug's lever is about 450 feet.

Under lateral motion there will be an additional dynamic load on the tugs' lines proportionate to the displacement of the ship and the ship's lateral velocity.

A potential swing to starboard has to be anticipated by checking lateral motion all the time. Once a rotational motion is on, there is rotational momentum. With a ship of this size, the resulting load can vastly exceed the backing power of the forward tug and the breaking strength of its lines if the tug falls too heavily into them.

It can be seen that the tug is at an advantage when made fast as far forward as it can safely work.

In the situation described, there is little or no safety margin. We would not willingly take the ship in under this condition, particularly not with a current from aft; however, with a 20-knot wind, on coming in, a sudden increase in wind speed from 20 to 25 knots may occur when the ship is already committed to the berth.

In figure 24 we are on board a tanker of 70,000 dwt, in ballast, in a following wind of 30 knots. We want to bring the ship to a stop by working the engine astern. The numbers from 1 to 8 indicate the positions the ship passes through under the effect of momentum, wind, and stern power. The numbered positions are discussed below:

1. The ship is moving ahead through the water at a speed of 6 knots, engine is stopped, telegraph is on full astern.

2. Engine working full astern. Transverse thrust of the propeller working astern has maximal leverage during forward motion in pushing the stern to port. Put at 5 percent of the applied stern power of the propulsion force, the transverse thrust comes up to a force of about 8 tons.

3. With the wind on the starboard quarter we have now the combined forces of wind and transverse thrust canting the ship to starboard.

4. The transverse component of the wind-force increases as the ship comes more beam to the wind. Lateral resistance at the port bow has pushed the pivot point back.

Following Wind

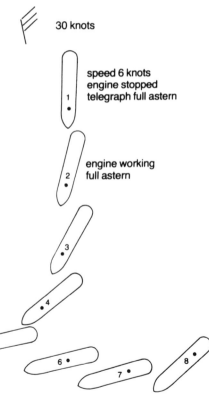

30 knots

speed 6 knots
engine stopped
telegraph full astern

engine working
full astern

Fig. 24. Following wind

43

5. The ship is stopped in the water, transverse wind-force is at maximum. The ship moves sideways to port.

6. When the ship gathers sternway, the pivot point moves sternward. The ship moves straight astern as long as transverse thrust and transverse wind-force balance.

7. With the pivot point well aft of the midship, a swing to port sets in. The product of wind-force and distance to pivot point is more than the product of transverse thrust and distance to pivot point (fig. 25). Transverse thrust at this stage can be put at 10 percent of applied stern power.

8. The more sternway the faster the swing to port. The moment of transverse wind-force increases and the moment of the transverse thrust decreases as the pivot point travels farther aft.

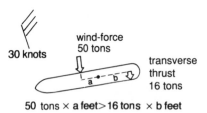

50 tons × a feet > 16 tons × b feet

Fig. 25. Beam wind versus transverse thrust.

Wind and CBM

As a 70,000-dwt tanker comes into a sea berth against a 20-knot wind, the wind-force constitutes a 23-ton load at the moment the ship is beam to the wind. The winch on the poop deck exerts a force of 15 tons, the winch on the main deck 12 tons. There is a backup force of about 10 tons exerted by three mooring launches pushing, in a combined effort, on the starboard quarter. The distance to the buoy is such that two lines had to be joined with a lashing to reach the buoy. The critical position arrives when the lashing comes to the barrel of the winch. If one line surges over the barrel, all the weight is on the other line. Much depends on how long it takes the crew on the poop deck to clear the lashing over the barrel of the winch, as the winch on the main deck plus the mooring launches cannot hold the ship against the wind.

When we have a good engine response, we can assist the operation by coming ahead on full right rudder, immediately followed by astern on the engine. We need good communication with the officer on the fantail to make sure that the propeller is clear when we use the engine.

Under stern motion, the pivot point will be aft, and the transverse wind-force tends to assist the swing into the berth. A strain on the port chain at this stage is very undesirable as it increases the load on the lines aft by stopping stern motion as well as by arresting the swing into the berth.

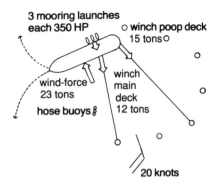

Fig. 26. Winch force versus wind-force.

A 250,000-dwt turbine tanker, loaded, is moving through the water at a speed of 1 knot. The 32,000-HP engine is stopped. A strong wind of 30 knots on the beam makes the ship swing to port. The rudder is full right. We are not in a position where we can go any faster. What do we do to stop the swing? We try a kick ahead. Just a kick. No result. Why?

Because we do not want to increase the speed, we have the engine on ahead for only a short while. It makes little difference whether we put the telegraph on full or on half because of the short length of time it will be on. The turbine will not come over 40 revs anyway. This gives us only about 2,000 HP. Let us assume that 50 percent of the thrust will go into the transverse rudder force. This gives us 50 percent of 20 tons, or 10 tons lift on the stern.

Let us further assume that the pivot point is at 0.3 L from the bow, wind-force at 0.5 L from the bow, and the rudder force at 1 L from the bow. This gives us:

Beam Wind on Loaded VLCC

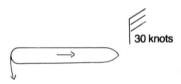

Fig. 27. Beam wind on loaded VLCC.

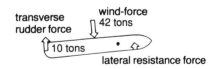

Fig. 28. Rudder force versus wind-force.

45

42 × 0.2 L which is more than 10 × 0.7 L,
or, the moment of the wind-force is more
than the moment of the rudder force. This
is why the kick ahead on full right rudder
did not stop the swing to port. (The lateral
resistance force at the starboard bow is
also helping the swing to port.)

What will happen when we put the engine on astern? When the speed comes off,
the pivot point will move sternward, and
the moment of the wind-force will be reduced to zero when the ship is stopped in
the water. At that time, the effect of the
beam wind will result in lateral motion.
We will see that the transverse thrust of
the propeller cants the stern to windward
before the ship comes to a full stop.

Wind and Single Buoy Mooring

In a position close to the monobuoy, when
the ship's relative speed to the buoy must
be zero, it is helpful to have a head current because motion through the water
keeps the pivot point forward. We must
prevent a situation from developing where
the ship moves astern through the water.
As sternway moves the pivot point sternward, it gives the transverse wind-force
more leverage. With a strong wind on the
bow it is then difficult, if not impossible,
to keep the ship in a position of imbalance.

If there is no current, we come in with
a minimal speed. To keep the ship steady,
we use judicious kicks ahead on full rudder. At zero speed, part of the propulsion
force will be absorbed by inertia, another
part by the longitudinal forces of wind
and sea. At the time of all secured, the
ship will probably sheer away from the
buoy and here again, we can use ahead on
the engine on full rudder. The advantage
of full rudder is not only that part of the
propulsion force is diverted and conse-

quently is not used for head motion, but also that the transverse rudder force helps in keeping the pivot point forward, checking the lever of the transverse wind-force (fig. 29). By turning into the wind, we reduce the magnitude of the transverse wind-force at the same time, and in this way we bring the ship up gently without putting a shock load on the mooring hawser.

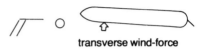

transverse wind-force

Fig. 29. Heading into the wind, speed zero.

When wind and tide are from different directions, there must be a balance between wind and tide to keep the ship in close proximity to the buoy long enough to secure the vessel. In figure 30, a VLCC, in ballast, is making the approach heading somewhere between the direction of wind and tide. The distance to the buoy is about a ship's length, speed over the ground is half a knot (according to the Doppler indicator), the ship is slightly swinging to starboard, rudder is hard left, and the engine stopped.

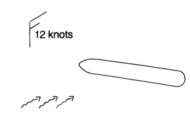

12 knots

Fig. 30. Wind and tide from different directions.

Instead of giving a kick ahead on full left rudder, we do better to take off all speed and see what the ship will do when the Doppler indicates zero speed over the ground. If there is no, or little current, the bow will be blown to port. This means that near the buoy we will also not be able to maintain this heading, and we will have to swing more to starboard, into the wind. As we still have enough distance to the buoy, we can come ahead on full right rudder and diminish the wind angle.

If, on the other hand, the ship remains steady at zero speed over the ground, it means that the ship is moving ahead through the water. In that case the pivot point is still forward, and, as we will be in the same situation near the buoy, we can continue our approach to the buoy on the same heading.

To let the ship swing to port we let the wind blow the bow down when the ship moves astern through the water. In the final stage of approach when the buoy is lost sight of under the bow, the rate-of-turn indicator is particularly useful in giving an early indication of rotational motion.

The best indicator for wind direction and wind-force is a flag flying at the mast or at some place up over the wheelhouse. By night, however, it may be difficult to see this flag, and at such time a speed/direction wind indicator is very helpful.

In figure 31, we can see how wind and tide have struck a balance with the mooring force to keep the ship beam to wind.

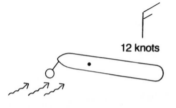

12 knots

Fig. 31. Wind and tide balance.

48

CHAPTER FOUR

Bow Thruster, Tugs

Shiphandling is rather a play of forces which are transmitted from the tug to the tow and vice versa, and these forces vary in direction, intensity, and duration. Shiphandling means basically transmitting impulses.
—W. Baer, *Assessment on Tug Performance*

Le manoeuvrier joue avec des forces sans cesse variables qui se combinent entre elles d'une infinité de façons.
—Pierre Célérier, *La Manoeuvre des Navires*

The bow thruster moves the water from one side of the bow to the other through a tunnel. The effect on a ship dead in the water and not exposed to other forces is that the foreship moves over. Due to the shape of the ship and the position of the tunnel, the ship pivots about a point that is approximately one ship's beam distance from the stern, as long as the ship makes no appreciable headway.

Fig. 32. Bow thruster.

To find out how the ship is affected by the use of the bow thruster we consider the effect of the force exerted by the bow thruster on the center of gravity with respect to the pivot point. With the initial pivot point at one ship's beam from the stern when the ship is dead in the water, the center of gravity is pushed over in the same direction in which the bow is moving. Because the direction of the rotational motion is in the same direction as

Effect of Bow Thruster

bow thruster force

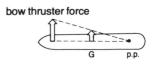

G   p.p.

Fig. 33. Effect of lateral thrust.

the lateral motion, lateral resistance is opposing the swing.

In order to produce thrust, the impeller in the tunnel has to build up a substantial flow of water. Rotational inertia has to be overcome before the swing sets in, and when it does, it has often been observed that the ship also starts creeping ahead. The cause of the very slight head motion could be the initial flow of water from ahead of the ship into the tunnel.

The direct control over the bow thruster from the bridge makes it very handy to use. This is probably the reason that there is a tendency to overuse the bow thruster to such an extent that it is working continuously, either to one side or to the other.

When the bow thruster is used instead of the rudder for turning the ship, it should be realized that bow thruster and rudder have a different effect on the ship. The forces of bow thruster and rudder are exerted on opposite ends of the ship: the bow thruster moves the foreship directly over in the direction of the desired swing, whereas the rudder moves the stern away in order to move the foreship in the direction of the desired swing. Moreover, under forward motion of the ship, the useful effect of the bow thruster decreases whereas the transverse rudder force is not affected by forward motion. Of even more consequence to the maneuver is the shift in position of the pivot point as a result of the introduction of a force at the forward end of the ship. The bow thruster in conjunction with the rudder can either turn the ship quickly or move the ship sideways by working in the same direction (Appendix B, 6).

As the bow thruster is most effective when the ship is dead in the water, we use full rudder and limited engine power to

50

keep the ship's speed down. With increase in forward motion the bow thruster is easily outbalanced by the rudder force. On ships with the possibility of 40 degrees of rudder or, better still, 45 degrees of rudder, it is worthwhile to insist on full rudder, as the man at the wheel may routinely give only 35 degrees. When we want to move the ship laterally without causing headway, it is important to increase the transverse rudder force at the expense of the longitudinal force which would otherwise result in a detrimental effect on the bow thruster force.

Some ships have the control and revolutions indicator of the bow thruster on the bridgewing so that we can check if the bow thruster is working or not. It also gives us an indication of how much we get. When the controls are in the wheelhouse, the shiphandler on the bridgewing has no certainty of what he gets.

Comparing the Effect of Rudder and Bow Thruster

To demonstrate the difference in effect of rudder and bow thruster we consider the effect of both on the center of gravity with respect to the pivot point while the ship is dead in the water (fig. 34). By using the rudder for a swing to port, the center of gravity G moves to starboard, whereas when we use the bow thruster for a swing to port, the center of gravity moves to port. The stern moves over in the first case and the bow in the second case.

The effect of the underwater resistance will be different when the ship starts moving ahead through the water, and the center of lateral resistance moves forward. Under increased longitudinal motion the lateral resistance grows in almost direct proportion to the rudder force and contributes to the swing; the lateral resistance

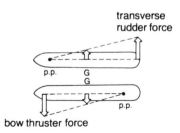

Fig. 34. Ship dead in the water.

51

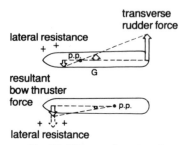

Fig. 35. Ship moving ahead
at very slow speed.

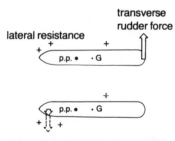

Fig. 36. Effect of rudder and bow
thruster under speed.

force works in the same direction as the swing.

When we use the bow thruster for a swing to port, we give the ship lateral motion to port and the resultant lateral resistance is opposing the bow thruster force. Forward motion brings the center of lateral resistance forward, and increase in speed through the water increases the lateral resistance. Only part of the underwater resistance is absorbed by the intake of the bow thruster tunnel. Consequently, the bow thruster loses in effect with increase in speed as it decreases in both magnitude and leverage.

As the underwater resistance is directly proportionate to the ship's speed, it follows that the resultant bow thruster force is inversely proportionate to the ship's speed.

At full speed the bow thruster force may have an opposite effect on the center of gravity, moving it away from the swing when the pivot point comes between the resultant bow thruster force and the center of gravity. However, the bow is meeting very strong underwater resistance, leaving a small resultant bow thruster force to push the bow over and to move the stern up against the lateral resistance abaft the pivot point (fig. 36). On a ship under speed the bow thruster force is exerted too close to the center of lateral resistance and is too small in comparison with the underwater resistance to have a noticeable effect. Moreover, the water rushing past the apertures of the tunnel greatly reduces the useful effect.

A tug pushing in the same direction and at the same position as the bow thruster has the same diminishing effect with increase of forward motion of the ship. The tug may have difficulty in maintaining

52

position as well. Increase in ship's speed makes it increasingly more difficult to remain at right angles to the ship. If not perpendicularly applied, the tug's force loses out in transverse force which further reduces the net lateral effect.

The bow thruster is very effective in steering the ship under sternway because the bow thruster has effective leverage with the pivot point aft. Moreover, the lateral resistance on the exposed quarter is assisting the swing.

The rotational effect of the transverse thrust of the propeller can easily be overcome by the bow thruster (or a tug). With a good sternway on and the controlling force of the bow thruster forward, it makes not much difference whether the propeller is right- or left-handed. By keeping the bow a bit to port, we can easily counteract the rotational effect of a right-handed propeller; for a left-handed propeller we keep the bow a bit to starboard.

In stern-first dockings, the bow thruster is an excellent aid, giving us almost perfect control over the bow while the ship is under sternway. As it is easier to kill sternway by coming ahead on the engine than it is to stop a ship under headway, stern-first docking is, in principle, safer than head-in docking.

Under consideration we have a 50,000-dwt tanker in loaded condition, portside-to docking, coming in very slowly. For the sake of interest we consider the effect of using the bow thruster/forward tug as compared to using the rudder. What will happen when we use rudder and propeller

Effect of Bow Thruster During Sternway

bow thruster force   lateral resistance

Fig. 37. Bow thruster under sternway.

Rudder or Bow Thruster/Tug

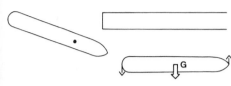

Fig. 38. Rudder/propeller effect.

Fig. 39. Effect of using bow thruster/forward tug.

and how will the ship behave when we use bow thruster/forward tug?

By using the rudder and engine (fig. 38), we create not only rotational—but also longitudinal—and lateral motion. Under lateral motion the loaded ship develops side momentum which moves the ship away from the finger pier. Rotational momentum sweeps the stern away from the dock and will be hard to stop, especially on the loaded ship. On coming astern on the engine, the transverse thrust of the propeller counters the rotational motion. However, the transverse thrust is not strong enough to stop the ship from moving away from the dock laterally. The result of using rudder and propeller is that the ship comes in too far from the dock and too close to the ship alongside the next finger pier.

Instead of using rudder and propeller, from the same position, we will now use the bow thruster for lining up the ship for the finger pier (fig. 39). We can expect a good effect of the bow thruster at this low speed; a forward tug may initially increase the ship's forward motion when coming up at right angles to the ship's side.

A transverse force exerted forward on the ship brings the bow in and counteracts lateral motion away from the pier, which would otherwise result from a turn to port. The continued push on the bow also tends to push the pivot point sternward, and consequently, when the speed is taken off by coming astern on the engine, the transverse thrust of the propeller will have reduced leverage. If the stern comes in more than anticipated, we can give a kick ahead on full left rudder when the speed has come off, or, depending on how far the ship is off the dock, we can use the bow thruster to port and stop rotational motion by diverting it into lateral motion. Lateral motion comes off sooner than rotational motion and results in a flat landing.

Again we have a 50,000-dwt tanker, in a loaded condition for a portside-to docking. We will observe the ship's behavior under the effect of using rudder and propeller or bow thruster/forward tug.

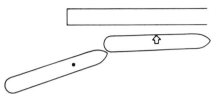

Fig. 40. Effect of using rudder/propeller.

The speed of approach and the angle of approach will determine if we need a cant to starboard before coming astern on the engine (fig. 40). The transverse thrust of the propeller will aggravate the cant of the stern to port in case the swing was already on. Side momentum moves the ship toward the dock while the stern moves in faster than the bow. The transverse thrust is having a strong rotational effect as long as the ship is moving ahead and the pivot point is forward. We can anticipate a stronger transverse thrust on a motorship with a big slow-turning propeller.

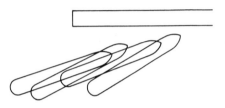

Fig. 41. Bow thruster effect.

We must judge correctly when the speed must be off altogether and be prepared to give a kick ahead on full left rudder if the stern moves in too fast. Full rudder angle is very important when we want to stop rotational motion: the more longitudinal propulsion force is deflected into transverse rudder force, the sooner we stop the swing without appreciable acceleration of forward motion of the ship.

The effect of the bow thruster moves the bow alternately in and out; the stern is not coming closer to the dock (fig. 41). On full astern there is practically no effect of the transverse thrust of the propeller as the pivot point has moved sternward under the effect of the transverse force exerted on the bow (Appendix B, 6).

Unjustified use of the bow thruster can be counterproductive. In a case like this, we better not use the bow thruster/forward tug until the final stage of docking when we need a force forward to balance the forces fore and aft to keep the ship parallel to the dock.

In the foregoing cases we do not consider the use of the after tug. Where we use a kick ahead on full rudder, we do so in practice on a motor ship when we need a quick response. We need the after tug in combination with the tug forward when the ship's motion is influenced by the effect of shallow water, current, or a strong wind.

Comparing Use of Tug and Bow Thruster

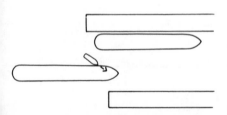

Fig. 42. Restriction in space reduces efficiency of tug.

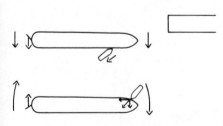

Fig. 43. Tug pushing or pulling at an angle.

Assisting tugs may cause unwanted lateral motion, sometimes resulting in unwanted rotational motion, when alongside the ship underway to the berth; they push against the ship's side when their line is not yet made fast, and they push even more while picking up the slack of their line on making fast. Once alongside, a tug is likely to push when the ship's side is not flush.

Tugs may cause unwanted longitudinal motion when the assisted ship has too much headway, which makes it difficult for the tug to come at right angles; part of the tug's power is spent on increasing headway while the tug is trying to come to position. Also, when there is not enough room for the tug to come at right angles, the tug is shoving ahead while trying to push the ship in (fig. 42).

An advantage of the tug over the bow thruster is that it can reduce the ship's speed while pulling or pushing the assisted ship (fig. 43). A limiting factor for the tug is the safe working load of the line and the vulnerability of the line; there is a lapse of time while the tug is gently putting weight on the line.

A nozzle increases the tug's output and brings the bollard pull on ahead up to about 130 percent of what it would be without a nozzle. But then the tug can give only half that pull on astern. Moreover, a pull on the line not in a horizontal direction loses out horizontally. In addition, there is a further loss when the tug's wash is directed against the side of the assisted ship.

The advantage of the bow thruster is the instantaneous availability of a force equal in both directions. However, the direction of the bow thruster force is only on the beam. In case of restricted space, the bow thruster has a definite advantage over a tug on the bow. Too much headway of the ship causes loss of efficiency of both tug and bow thruster.

We consider a 50,000-dwt tanker, in ballast condition, ready to sail. In coming astern on the engine, the transverse thrust of the propeller keeps the stern alongside the pier. In order not to damage the fendering of the pier and the ship's paint, we will try to keep the ship away from the pier.

We can pull the stern off by backing the after tug (fig. 44). Initially, the pivot point will be forward as long as the ship has no sternway. When we use the engine on astern, the pivot point will move aft, and the transverse thrust will exert a force toward the dock. When there is no wind, the ship will move toward the dock, but with a wind on the starboard bow, the foreship will be blown in, and the bow may rake the pier. For that reason we like to keep the ship more parallel to the pier. This can be achieved by letting the after tug pull the ship out alongside (fig. 45).

Tug and Pivot Point

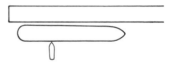

Fig. 44. Pulling the stern off.

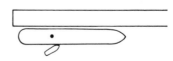

Fig. 45. Pulling the ship out by the tug alongside.

This works out nicely on a ballasted ship which is trimmed, say 10 feet, by the stern. Under sternway, the pivot point will not move too far aft because of the trim. The ship will initially move away from the dock, and, on gathering speed, move parallel to the pier; we can use the engine on astern without being too much affected by the transverse thrust.

On a loaded tanker on even keel, however, the pivot point moves farther aft and may settle aft of the point of impact of the after tug, especially when the chock through which the tug's line is taken is halfway between the accommodation aft and the ship's manifold. In this case we see the stern coming back in before the ship is clear of the finger pier. We can forestall this by letting the tug pull the ship off under an angle of 45 degrees. With limited bottom clearance on the bigger loaded tankers we let the after tug pull on the beam to lift the stern off before coming astern on the engine (fig. 44).

Tugs, Wind, and Pivot Point

A 70,000-dwt tanker, in ballast, draft 16 by 26 feet, is to dock stern-first, starboard alongside. In figure 46, the ship is moving ahead, pivot point forward; the ship has a tendency to move up into the wind. Tugs may push slightly to better position themselves. The forward tug works more or less as a bow thruster; the main difference is that the bow thruster would have equal power in both directions, whereas the tug is stronger in pushing than in backing. An initial swing to starboard, before coming astern on the engine, helps the maneuver.

This is the critical position (fig. 47). The pivot point moves sternward when the ship gathers sternway. The forward

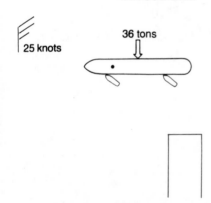

25 knots

36 tons

Fig. 46. Wind on the beam.

58

tug must be pushing full before the ship comes to this position so that a good swing to starboard is on before the wind catches the bow. The after tug swings round on the propeller wash, and we can let it pull when it is helpful. The tug develops less power backing, and the moment of this force decreases as the pivot point comes aft. The transverse force of the propeller grows stronger when sternway sets in but reduces in rotational effect when the pivot point comes farther aft.

The magnitude of the transverse wind-force decreases as the ship comes more head to wind, but as the pivot point moves aft, the distance of this force to the pivot point has increased and the moment of the wind-force may increase if the swing to starboard is too slow (fig. 48).

The after tug has difficulties staying in a good position because of propeller wash. The transverse thrust of the propeller decreases when we slow down on the engine on astern. The longitudinal wind-force increases in strength.

The rotational motion to starboard should be entirely stopped by now (fig. 49). In case rotational momentum moves the foreship farther over, we will have the wind on the port bow and a transverse wind-force to starboard. With the pivot point well aft, the moment of the transverse wind-force will grow rapidly if the tug is late in checking the swing. The tug must then pull on the rope and we must not only rely on the breaking strength and the condition of the rope, but also on the tug skipper's skill in gently coming up into the rope. It is safer to have the tug in a position where the tug must push. For that reason we keep the bow out a bit while the ship is backing and leave a small transverse wind-force pushing on

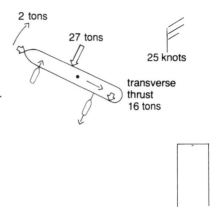

Fig. 47. Wind 60° on the bow.

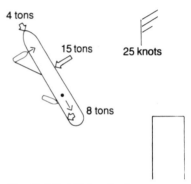

Fig. 48. Wind 30° on the bow.

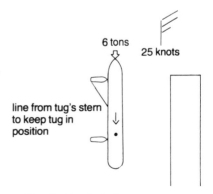

Fig. 49. Head wind.

the starboard bow which can easily be controlled by the forward tug.

Use of Tugs

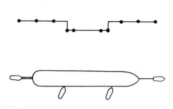

Fig. 50. Tugs assisting ULCC.

On the Hook

The forward tug is on the hawser taken through the center lead forward (fig. 50). When the assisted ship is dead in the water or practically stopped, the tug can come on the beam. It takes time to shift from port to starboard and vice versa. During the final stage of docking this tug pulls out on the beam to control the lateral motion in.

Alongside

The tug is good for pushing. Ballasted ships with a high freeboard give a bad lead for pulling. Sea condition may make it difficult or impossible to work alongside without damaging the tug's fenders or breaking the tug's rope.

As Tractor

As on the hook, but the lines are made fast forward on the tug. The advantage of taking off the speed of the assisted ship with tug aft is twofold: a quicker response and a better directional control. During the final stage of docking, this tug also pulls out on the beam to control the lateral motion in.

CHAPTER FIVE

Current

*I do not disparage theory in any way because
it is an asset, but to theory must be added
practical experience which sometimes proves
theory to be wrong.*
  —W. Bartlett Prince, *Pilot, Take Charge*

Theory does not always work out in practice.
  —Malcolm C. Armstrong, *Practical
  Shiphandling*

Wind and current are usually associated
as both being forces not under control of
the shiphandler. The two forces have, however, a different effect on the ship because
of the difference in nature of the two.
When the ship is affected by wind alone
and moves through the water, the hull
meets underwater resistance. When, on
the other hand, the ship's motion origi-
nates from current, there is practically no
resistance of the above-water area to air.
As water is eight hundred times denser
than sea level atmosphere, current must,
by nature, have considerably stronger effect than wind, especially on loaded ships.

Current has a direct effect on the underwater part of the ship and an indirect effect expressed in momentum after the
ship alters course or comes out of a current, when the ship will carry momentum
in the direction of the current that the
ship was previously subjected to.

Whereas the effect of wind on the ship has
to be considered with respect to the pivot

Effect of Wind and Current

61

point, current affects a freely moving ship as a whole and consequently its effect is on the center of gravity. However, when we try to keep the ship stationary relative to the ground, we must arrest the ship's movement and let the ship make speed through the water contrary to the current, in which case the ship meets underwater resistance.

All freely moving ships, not being subjected to wind and dead in the water, have the same speed as the current, whether the ships are big or small, loaded or light. Ships not freely moving, as ships at anchor or moored, are subjected to pressure exerted by the current, pressure which is directly proportionate to the exposed underwater area and to the square of the current velocity.

In a strong tide we see that ships at anchor, or moored to a single point, are heading into the tide; when it is nearly slack water ballasted ships will be more affected by wind while the loaded tankers still remain heading into the tide. When we approach the monobuoy with a ballasted tanker in wind and tide condition, the direction of the loaded tankers, moored on single points nearby, gives us an indication of the direction of the current. However, the heading of the ballasted ship, after having been tied up to the buoy, may be quite different from the heading of the loaded ship (fig. 31).

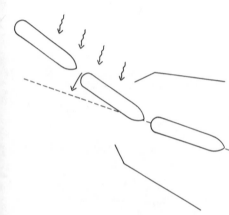

Fig. 51. Entering a sheltered port.

Effect of Partial Exposure to Current

Current can have a turning effect on the ship when only part of the ship is exposed to current, as, for instance, a ship entering a sheltered port where the after part of the ship is still exposed to current that runs outside the port and the foreship is already in sheltered water (fig. 51).

By making the approach from up current and under an angle, we can compensate for the effect of current. The current assists in pushing the stern down and getting the ship in the leading line.

On making the approach with a slow moving, deeply loaded tanker, we must take into account side momentum in the direction of the current which continues on when the ship gets out of the current.

There will be no turning effect when the ship is subjected to an even flow of current and is allowed to float freely without being hampered by outside forces. It is when we try to keep the ship in the same position relative to a berth that the vessel is meeting underwater resistance.

Let us consider a starboard side-to docking in a current that comes in on the starboard quarter. Two tugs are alongside, one forward, one aft, trying to keep the ship parallel to the dock. Remaining in the same position relative to the dock, the ship is, in fact, moving through the water and meeting underwater resistance. The center of lateral resistance is well abaft amidships because of sternway through the water. When the tugs push with equal power, the ship will swing to starboard; not because the current turns the ship, but because the pivot point is aft and the distance of the forward tug to the pivot point is longer than the distance of the after tug to the pivot point. Without the tugs pushing there would be no lateral motion and no swing; the ship would move with the current and make no speed through the water, but would move relative to the dock.

The after tug gives mainly lateral motion and no turning motion as long as the

Fully Exposed to Current

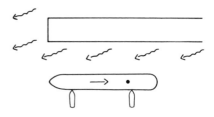

Fig. 52. Docking against a current from aft.

ship is under sternway. In order to keep the ship parallel to the dock, we must keep the forward tug stopped.

Magnitude of Current Force on the Beam

The load exerted by a current on the beam of a stationary vessel can be enormous because the load is directly proportionate to the exposed underwater area and the square of the speed of the current. For our purpose, a general idea about the magnitude of the force of a beam current is good enough, and the following formula may be used:

$$C = f \times L \times d \times v^2$$

where: C = current load in short tons

L = length in feet at waterline

d = mean draft

v = current speed in knots

In this formula, f is a factor which depends on the underkeel clearance; it varies from 0.0015, when the depth of water is 3 times the draft, to 0.0036, when the depth is 1.1 times the draft; when the depth of water is 2 times the draft, the factor is 0.0018.

Example

What is the load exerted by a beam current of 1 knot, 2 knots, and 3 knots on a tanker of 70,000 dwt? Length at waterline 790 feet; depth of water 46 feet.

Using the formula above we find that with the ship in ballast, mean draft 21 feet, the load exerted by a current on the beam will be about 30 tons in a 1-knot current, 120 tons in a 2-knot current, and 270 tons in a 3-knot current. In loaded condition, draft 42 feet, the load exerted will be respectively: 120 tons, 480 tons, 1,075 tons.

Wind and Current in a CBM

A tanker berthing in a CBM (conventional buoy mooring) with deep draft, may have a struggle coming in, when there is a current across the berth. A beam wind has generally less effect, even on a light ship, than a beam current. To illustrate this point, we will consider the effect of a beam current of 0.7 knots and a beam wind of 12 knots on a 90,000-dwt tanker.

In light condition, mean draft 20 feet, the current exerts a load of 12 tons, and the 12-knot wind a load of 9 tons, which makes for a total transverse force of 21 tons. If the tanker comes in with part cargo, 35,000 tons, 35 feet mean draft, the current will exert a force of 25 tons, and the wind-force will be 6 tons, bringing the total transverse wind-force up to 31 tons.

We are lucky to get three lines out quickly in the position (fig. 53), for now we depend on the line handling skill of the crew, on the correct position of the fairleads, bitts, and winches, and on the capacity of the winches. When the winches can exert a force of 15 tons each and not too much of this force is lost on bad leads, we have enough power to hold the ship against wind and current. The combined forces of the mooring launches pushing on the port side facilitate stopping off and belaying the lines.

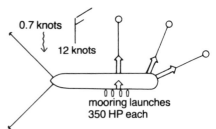

mooring launches
350 HP each

90,000 dwt	LOA = 810 feet
B = 128 feet	LBP = 785 feet
D = 58 feet	L = 800 feet

Fig. 53. Mooring against wind and current.

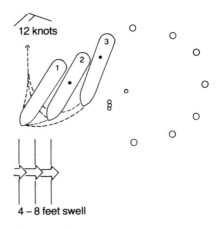

Fig. 54. Effect of swell.

On an open roadstead, where the ship is exposed to swell, we experience the effect of swell as being similar to the effect of current. Coming in with a 46,000-dwt turbine tanker, in ballast, bridge midships, into a conventional seaberth and having dropped both anchors in the right position (fig. 54, 1), we try to back the ship as fast as possible.

Poor stern power, in this case, allows the swell to set the ship in quickly (fig. 54, 2). As the pivot point comes aft while the ship

Effect of Swell

65

is backing, the bow is blown down by the wind (fig. 54, 3).

No strain on the starboard chain is due to the poor heaving rate of the windlass (1 shot/4 minutes). A good windlass would have been able to recover the slack on the starboard chain quick enough for a resulting strain on the chain to hold the bow. The launches cannot assist because of swell.

Current and Momentum

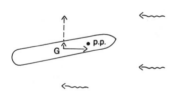

Fig. 55. Side motion resulting in side momentum.

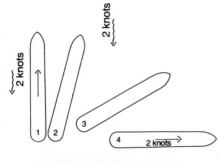

Fig. 56. Longitudinal momentum after course alteration in current.

A head current allows us to use engine power for steering without developing speed over the ground. The ship can proceed at a speed through the water equal to the speed of the current and stay in the same position relative to the ground or to a dock, as long as the current is dead ahead. When the ship cants to either side, there will be a transverse component of the ship's motion which can be used to advantage to move the ship sideways. When the side motion is on for some length of time, we must be prepared for side momentum (fig. 55), especially on a loaded ship.

To stop the side motion we can take the current on the opposite bow, but we must do that well in time, for the ship has to move farther sideways before it will take effect. This is due to the fact that we have to move the center of gravity over with respect to the pivot point before the opposite side of the hull will be exposed to the current.

A ship stemming a tide of 2 knots (fig. 56, 1) makes a speed through the water of 2 knots. When the ship swings beam to the tide, the ship still makes a speed through the water of 2 knots (fig. 56, 4), but now also over the ground. The ship is shooting ahead, even when the engine is stopped, because of longitudinal momentum.

On a big loaded tanker it can be an un-
pleasant surprise to find oneself with an
unexpected longitudinal speed of 2 knots.
With a change in ship's heading in a current we must be aware of momentum. In
order to better anticipate momentum after course alteration, information from instrument readings on speed—over the
ground as well as through the water—is
very helpful.

It can happen that the current is not
equally strong over the whole width of the
waterway or the path of approach to a
berth.

A ship proceeding against a current of 2
knots with a speed through the water of 3
knots (fig. 57, 1), makes a speed over the
ground of 1 knot. When the ship comes
over to where the current runs at only 1
knot (fig. 57, 3), the ship is proceeding
with a speed over the ground of 2 knots,
also when the engine had been stopped, in
which case the longitudinal momentum
would have carried the ship on.

An unexpected speed of 2 knots on a
loaded VLCC takes time to be taken off. A
lesser speed of the current close to a berth
can be the cause for too much speed in the
final stage of approach to a berth. On entering a sheltered port with a current running outside, we must make allowance for
momentum, especially on loaded ships.

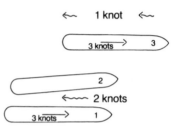

Fig. 57. Shooting ahead in
relatively weaker head current.

The current off San Nicolas, Aruba, can be
quite strong, up to 3 knots at times. It
drops gradually in strength during the
last stage of approach to the harbor entrance, and there may be a countercurrent
close to the entrance which builds up a
rough sea against the prevailing trade wind.
The direction of the current is westnorth-
west to northwesterly for most of the year.

Effect of Momentum on Entering a Sheltered Port

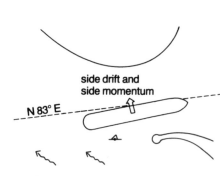

side drift and
side momentum

N 83° E

Fig. 58. Entering a sheltered port.

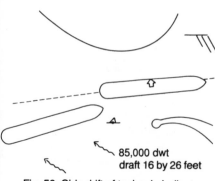

85,000 dwt
draft 16 by 26 feet

Fig. 59. Side drift of tanker in ballast.

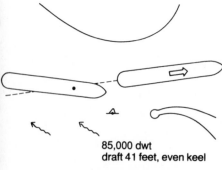

85,000 dwt
draft 41 feet, even keel

Fig. 60. Longitudinal momentum.

The drop in strength of the current during the last half-mile or so of the approach is especially noticeable on long ships, where 10 to 20 degrees of left rudder is on most of the time. When the ship's head enters sheltered water, the direct effect of the current is on the stern. The indirect effect of the momentum sets the ship bodily to port.

Smaller ships and tankers in ballast can come in from well south of the leading line and let the current and the 20/30-knot trade wind set the ship toward the leading line (fig. 59). The critical position is in the entrance. When current and wind are strong, the ship will have considerable side drift; we notice this by watching the leading line. The ship will swing to starboard because the after part is still subjected to current when the foreship is already sheltered. The bridge position aft moves over from south of the leading line to north of the leading line. We must assess the situation and decide whether we must stop the swing or let the ship swing more to starboard before giving left rudder. When the ship comes bodily over to port too fast, we not only let the swing to starboard continue, but also increase the engine revolutions in order not to touch the reef on our portside.

As their speed of approach is lower, the big loaded tankers are set down more by the drift of the current, and their approach tends to be heading more into the current. In this approach the pivot point is kept more or less on the leading line while adjusting the angle of drift (fig. 60). On entering port there will be less side momentum caused by current. Now, however, on getting out of the current, the ship will shoot ahead because of longitudinal momentum, and the impetus will be directly proportionate to the speed of the current.

Left rudder to turn the ship to port will counteract side momentum caused by current. As the big loaded tankers can be sluggish on low speed and have little bottom clearance, we may have to increase engine revolutions to have more thrust on the rudder.

As the big tankers require a long stopping distance, they have to go slowly; by going slowly, they are subjected longer to current. When the current is on the beam, we must cope with strong lateral momentum. If the ship is heading into the current, we must cope with longitudinal momentum once the ship gets out of the current.

As the room inside the inner harbor of San Nicolas is limited, the big loaded tankers are assisted by three tugs to take off the speed: one as tractor aft and one on each bow. The forward tugs can also assist in steering when we let only one tug back at a time. In case of a sheer, we let one tug push at the bow, while the other backs on the other bow.

An additional hazard is bank effect in the entrance, which can cause a sheer, but can also be used to advantage, when the vessel is correctly positioned (see Chapter 7).

Fig. 61. Tugs taking off speed by backing.

CHAPTER SIX

The Anchor

Considering anchoring in principle, the problem is to transfer a horizontal force acting on the ship at the surface, down to the seabed, where an equal and opposite resistance can be developed.
    —Mark Terrell, *Anchors—A New Approach*

The holding power of the anchor depends upon the nature of the bottom, the weight and shape of the anchor, and the amount of chain that is out. For maximum holding power, the shaft of the anchor should be flat on the bottom and, in order to obtain a horizontal pull, sufficient chain should be paid out.

At best, the holding power of the anchor itself, without the weight of the chain, is about four times its own weight. Thus, the holding power of a 15-ton anchor of a 70,000-dwt tanker is about a 60-ton load. When the shaft is lifted as to make an angle with the bottom of 5 degrees, the loss of holding power is 25 percent, and at 15 degrees the loss is about 50 percent. The chain contributes both to the weight and to the holding power of the anchor.

Dragging and Dredging

Even when the shaft of a 15-ton anchor is lifted from the bottom so as to make an angle of 5 degrees, there is, theoretically, still enough holding power to keep a 70,000-dwt tanker in a 60-knot head wind (fig. 62). In practice, however, we see that the ship starts yawing or weaving, which produces jerks on the chain that starts the anchor.

When the holding power of the anchor plus the chain is less than the force exerted on or by the ship, whether it be caused by the wind, current, or engine or by a combination of forces, the anchor will start to drag. When the anchor drags, it will still keep the ship head to wind. If the bottom allows us to do so, dredging the anchor is a safe and practical way of backing out without losing control over the bow. In the same way we can use the anchor for dredging when the ship is under headway. Dragging of the anchor is an unfortunate event brought about by the elements; dredging the anchor is done deliberately by using the engine and a short scope of chain.

The secret of successfully dredging the anchor is to keep a minimal speed over the ground and a constant strain on the chain. By moving very slowly, there is hardly any underwater resistance at the bow, and with very little strain on the chain, the pivot point stays pretty far forward.

The scope of chain is about 1½ times the distance from the hawsepipe to the bottom, which prevents the flukes from digging in. If the ship is allowed to develop speed over the ground, there is practically no effect of the anchor as it is dragged along over the bottom. The anchor on the the bottom has a good effect in minimizing the speed of a light ship. The momentum of the loaded ship, on the other hand, is difficult to control by the comparatively weak force exerted by the anchor being dredged.

It is only when the ship hardly moves that the pivot point stays forward resulting in a large swinging moment which makes the thrust of the propeller, turning at minimum revolutions, very effective on full rudder. It makes it possible to hold up

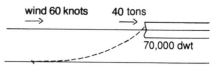

Fig. 62. Holding power of anchor.

71

the stern of a light ship against a beam wind, while the anchor holds the bow.

Conventional Buoy Mooring

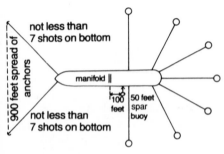

Fig. 63. Tanker of 70,000 dwt in CBM.

Today, when most berthings and unberthings are tug assisted, there is probably no better place to observe a ship's behavior than a sea berth, where no tugs are available. Here we practice shiphandling in its purest form. In a subtle way we have to avail ourselves of every windfall and opportunity to get the ship in the right direction. The anchor, an awkward but powerful piece of equipment, can assist us in our efforts, if used with skill and a little bit of luck.

In a conventional sea berth, the ship must be brought into a fixed position without the benefit of a solid structure to hold the ship in position. The ship's manifold must be a certain distance away from the end of the submarine pipeline; and when this position has been reached, the ship should be safely secured.

An advantage of a sea berth over a dock is that, except for the submarine pipeline, there are no unmoveable objects, and there is no risk of damage caused by impact. However, there are many objects floating around that can foul the propeller, and the propeller itself can play havoc among the hoses if one of the hose buoys is caught.

With two anchors spread to keep the foreship in position and the aftship tied up to seven buoys, the ship must be in the right position to connect the loading hoses to the ship's manifold.

If the ship is too far back into the berth and the manifold too close to the end of the submarine pipeline, the loading hose is liable to kink. If, on the other hand, the ship is too far out and all the chain has been paid out, there is no other way but to do it all over again, pick up the anchors, and make a new approach.

In order to have the anchors in the right position, a range of leading marks is set out for a ship of a certain length or tonnage. Bigger ships must have their anchors farther out to have the same amount of chain out, and for this reason their approach is outside of the leading line; in other words, they must keep the marks open. Ships smaller than the range is set out for, in particular ships that are short of chain, keep inside of the leading line and have the marks open to the other side.

Owing to drift the direction of the ship's heading is seldom straight to the leading marks. Whereas the bow and the stern may follow a zigzag pattern during the approach because of corrective action, the pivot point follows a more or less fluent line on or parallel to the leading line. We keep the pivot point in mind in order not to overshoot the marks. A case in point is when we use the rudder for speed reduction instead of using stern power.

The anchors are dropped at the intersection of the drop leads and the leading line (fig. 64). When we drop the first anchor, we must let go freely with the brake wide open, until at least 4 shots are out to guarantee a horizontal pull on the anchor. Checking the chain at 2 or even 3 shots results in dragging the anchor.

We need different targets for bridge amidships and bridge aft position. A bridge farther forward than normal, as for instance on "jumboized" ships, may need a correction on the bridge amidships mark. In regard to the anchors that must be on the marks, we have to imagine ourselves

Making the Approach to the CBM

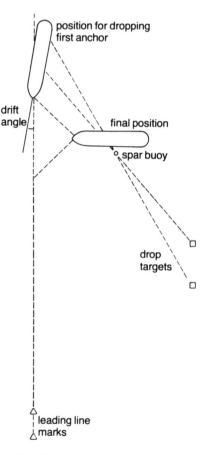

Fig. 64. Marks and drop targets in CBM.

73

on the fo'c'sle head while standing on the bridge. We deliberately put ourselves, on the bridge, off center in order to bring the bow in line and drop the anchor in the right place. The bridge aft makes it in no way easier to determine whether the bow is in line or not, especially for dropping the second anchor. The ship may have swung considerably at this stage and with our point of observation hundreds of feet away from the fo'c'sle head we have quite a different view on the marks.

Unfortunately, for this type of operation, the anchor has not evolved yet to a very high degree of efficiency and precision. It is in fact wishful thinking to rate the anchor with those forces under direct control of the shiphandler. With everything considered, it is probably safe to say that there is no job comparable to anchor work in a CBM, because the job involves guesswork and uncertainty in a situation which calls for precision.

There is no certainty that the anchor will drop at the moment we give the order to let go. For sure we may hear frantic hammering to release the brake, but the reassuring din of the chain rattling out may be seconds later. The result may be that the starboard anchor is not in the right position and that the anchors will not be sufficiently spread. This is especially the case when the ship has some speed on to offset a strong drift while letting go the first anchor. Also, we may ask ourselves whether the anchor will hold or drag. Is the chain slack or tight? How much is out? Here, it is the communication with the fo'c'sle head that is under the best of circumstances unsatisfactory. In this day and age, when we can have perfect communication with people walking on the moon, it is often not possible to communicate properly with people working on the bow of our own ship.

How is the chain leading? We are in the dark, hear a lot of noise, see a cloud of rust and dust, and hope for some kind of information. We need an experienced officer forward who has a very clear idea of what it is all about. For this operation depends to a large degree on the successful placing of the anchors and slacking of the chains. Not enough slack after letting go results in dragging the anchor across the berth, and too much slack piles the chain on the bottom, which may result in shortage of chain when the ship tries to move farther back into the berth. The cant to starboard to bring the ship into the berth can be assisted or arrested by holding on to the chain; the line handling aft can be hampered and endangered by keeping a strain on the chain at the wrong time.

After dropping the two anchors, the ship must be backed into the berth. The pivot point will be abaft the midship most of the time, at least when the ship is under sternway (fig. 65). Consequently, there is a small swinging moment for the transverse thrust of the propeller, but also when we give a kick ahead on full right rudder there is not much effect as long as the ship is backing.

On the other hand, the anchors have a large swinging moment when they have a good lead, the more on the beam the better. For this reason it is important to pick up the slack on the starboard chain when the port anchor has been dropped, and the ship is backing into the berth. A strain on the starboard chain assists the ship on turning into the berth. The port chain should be left slack.

Anchor and Swing

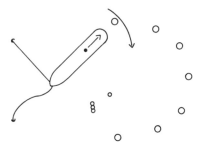

Fig. 65. Berthing: using a strain on the chain to advantage.

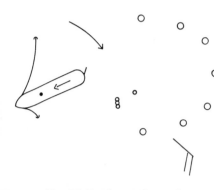

Fig. 66. Turning on the anchor.

On coming in against a strong wind we can use starboard anchor to swing the ship —after having let go the second anchor— before backing into the berth.

Provided the ship was dead in the water and the chain tight, very little strain is put on the starboard chain when we come ahead on 10 shots of chain and on full right rudder (fig. 66). We may have to increase the engine speed to half or even to full speed ahead to get the swing started (see Appendix B, 8). Most of the ship's propulsion force is spent on the swing against the wind, for when the swing sets in, the tension in the chain eases quickly.

Anchor and Position of Pivot Point

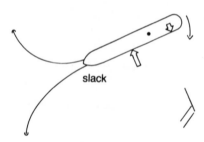

slack

Fig. 67. Wind effect when port chain is kept slack.

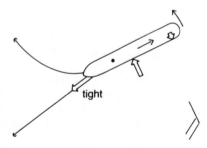

tight

Fig. 68. Wind effect when port chain is tight.

A wind across the berth will not stop the swing of the incoming ship as long as the ship is backing, and the port chain is kept slack (fig. 67). A strain on the port chain gives practically no turning effect in this stage as the chain is leading almost straight ahead. Holding onto the port chain, however, arrests the ship's sternway and reverses the ship's motion. This, in turn, brings the pivot point forward, and the turning effect of the wind will be contrary to the desired swing because the point of impact of the transverse wind-force will come abaft the pivot point (fig. 68). Instead of seeking the wind, the stern will be blown to leeward.

A kick ahead on full right rudder doesn't do much good either, as this also brings the pivot point forward. On a turbine-powered ship, it takes an especially long time before the engine is working astern and longer still before the ship starts moving astern and before the pivot point moves back aft again. With the pivot point forward the wind-force is working against the maneuver.

76

A ship that has the bridge amidships is easier to handle against a crosswind than a ship with the bridge aft.

With a fairly strong wind on the port bow we better keep control over the bow by not slacking too much on the port chain. The bow of the light ship is easily blown to starboard if there is too much slack on the port chain (fig. 69). When we are late in checking the port chain, it takes time to control the swing. By the time the chain comes sufficiently tight to pull its weight, the stern may have swept over the hose buoys. In this case it is easier to handle a ship with the bridge aft, where the windage aft gives a stabilizing effect in a head wind.

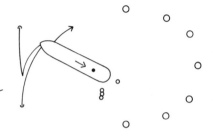

Fig. 69. Wind on the bow.

Leaving the CBM

It is interesting to observe the ship's behavior during the process of unmooring when we leave the sea berth under ideal weather conditions. Not influenced by wind or current, all the ship's movements are caused by the pull on the anchors, and the way the chains are laid out on the bottom. Since the ship is now fully loaded, inertia plays an important part; when motion is on, momentum comes into play.

Occasionally, we may have to use engine and rudder to relieve the strain on the chain, to prevent the stern from coming too near the hose buoys, or to try and prevent the chain from leading over the bulbous bow. However, we must bear in mind that the direction the chain is leading is not always the direction to the anchor on the bottom, and that the motion of the stern in one direction may result in motion of the bow in the opposite direction and vice versa. In most cases it is best to let the ship find her own way without using the engine too much and to stop

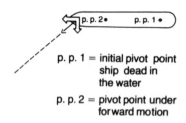

p. p. 1 = initial pivot point
ship dead in
the water

p. p. 2 = pivot point under
forward motion

Fig. 70. Effect of strain on the chain.

heaving just when the chain comes tight in order to prevent a windlass breakdown.

A strain on the chain transmits an impulse to the ship. The heaving rate of the windlass determines the duration of the impulse transmitted to the foreship and consequently the duration of the ensuing motion. The force exerted by the windlass gives the ship mainly rotational and longitudinal motion. The lateral motion ceases to have an effect as soon as the ship starts moving ahead (fig. 70). The pivot point then tends to come forward of the center of gravity. Moreover, any lateral motion that may have originated from the initial impulse meets strong underwater resistance in lateral direction when the ship is fully loaded.

After the lines are all let go, the ship moves ahead under the strain on both anchor chains. We start heaving on the port chain. The foreship moves toward the port anchor and causes the bight of the starboard chain to gradually lead astern. A strain develops on the starboard chain when there are about 4 shots more to go on port. The swing to port stops when the motion of the foreship is arrested by the strain on the starboard chain. At this moment, when both the anchor chains come tight, a breakdown in the windlass may occur, especially on older ships. To facilitate the heaving home of the port anchor we slack away on the starboard chain until at least the same amount of chain is out as the original spread between the two anchors. It will take a good windlass only four to five minutes to recover the 2 shots of chain that we have slacked off, and it may save us four to five hours of windlass repairs.

As soon as the port anchor is lifted from the bottom, it loses the grip it had on the bow. Then the sheer weight of the starboard chain catenary is seen to have effect: the ship moves astern and swings to starboard. In order to clear the hose buoys we come ahead on the engine and bring the ship gently up against the starboard chain. When the stern passes the hose buoys, we come full astern on the engine to continue the starboard swing and to take the weight off the chain. A slow windlass allows the starboard swing plenty of time to continue before any strain comes on the starboard chain. Meanwhile, the bow swings so far to starboard that the chain starts leading across the bow to port, which is particularly undesirable when the ship has a bulbous bow. The situation can be avoided if we leave the engine working astern a bit longer so that we can afford to come ahead on the engine on full left rudder to kill the swing to starboard and have the ship dead in the water.

A light breeze coming in from the port side is helpful in keeping the ship on the same side of the spar buoy. By giving plenty of slack on the starboard chain while heaving on the port chain, the ship comes so far ahead that the port chain starts leading to port. A strain on the port chain will give the bow a swing to port. In order to prevent a swing to starboard from developing when the port anchor comes aweigh, we come dead slow astern on the engine as soon as the port chain is up and down. Stern motion brings up the starboard chain growing ahead of the ship, and the drag of the chain dampens down a swing that may have been caused initially by the weight of the chain and the transverse thrust of the propeller working astern.

It usually takes some time before the starboard anchor windlass is put into gear and before the slack of the chain has been

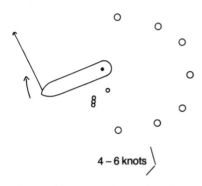

4 – 6 knots

Fig. 71. Transverse force of anchor.

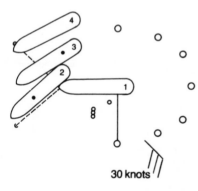

30 knots

Fig. 72. Strong wind on the port quarter.

picked up. Meanwhile, the stern motion gets lost and by the time the starboard chain comes tight, leading abeam, the ship is almost dead in the water (fig. 71).

The force of the windlass brings the bow over quickly, and the ensuing rotational motion has the pivot point very far aft. Although the stern seems to swing into the direction of the spar buoy, the ship does not come closer.

If there is still sternway on at this time, we give dead slow ahead on full left rudder; this will not appreciably affect the rotational motion because of the close proximity of the rudder force to the pivot point (see Appendix B, 6). The effect of trim is noticeable: the pivot point on the loaded tanker on even keel moves far aft under the effect of a transverse force exerted far forward on the ship. The only effect of engine and rudder is a lateral motion of the ship away from the spar buoy until both sternway and rotational momentum come off. At that moment the pivot point moves forward, and we can try to balance out windlass force and rudder force to move the ship laterally away from the spar buoy.

With a strong wind in on the port quarter, the last line to let go is the line from port main deck aft (fig. 72). We start heaving on the port chain as soon as the last line is let go, and the ship moves ahead. With the pivot point forward the stern is blown down faster than the foreship, and the ship comes beam to the wind (fig. 72, 2).

The forward motion dissipates, and the swing to port gradually comes to a stop, provided there is no strain on the chains. When the port anchor is aweigh, we come astern on the engine; stern motion brings

80

the pivot point sternward. Now it is the bow which is blown down (fig. 72, 3).

We give very little stern motion which is soon lost. The ship drifts bodily over to where the starboard anchor is on the bottom; while we heave away, the chain remains slack all the time, until it comes up and down.

If in position shown in figure 72, 2, the starboard chain is not slacked off in time, the ship will be held back, and the port chain will come tight (fig. 73). This causes the stern to be blown down rapidly, and the swing to port continues while we are heaving on the last shots of the port chain (fig. 73, 3).

When we are heaving on the starboard chain, the swing still continues (fig. 73, 4). By the time the starboard anchor is aweigh, the ship is heading in the wrong direction (fig. 73, 5).

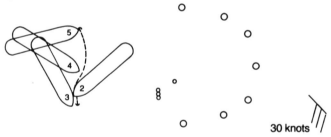

Fig. 73. Making complete turn due to strain on chain.

Stern motion brings the pivot point sternward, and the wind will blow the bow farther to port, continuing the swing. The ship will end up having made a complete turn, taking more time and more strain on the chain than during the procedure followed in figure 72.

On leaving the sea berth, after loading, with a strong wind in from starboard, we hold on to the line from the main deck

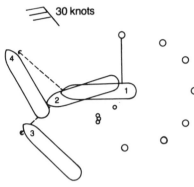

Fig. 74. Wind on starboard bow on leaving the berth.

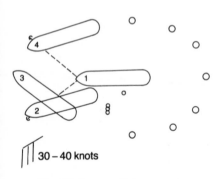

Fig. 75. Strong wind on port bow on leaving the berth.

starboard (fig. 74). Just before letting go this line we give a kick ahead on full left rudder in order to clear the spar buoy and the hose buoys (fig. 74, 2).

It takes time before the wind-force overcomes the rotational momentum of the loaded ship. Meanwhile, we take in the last rope and heave away on the port chain. The forward motion keeps the pivot point forward and the stern is blown down (fig. 74, 3). By keeping a strain on the chain while heaving on starboard, we keep the ship head to wind (fig. 74, 4).

A very strong wind on the port bow, on leaving the berth, creates a dangerous situation at the moment when the port anchor is up, and we start heaving on the starboard (fig. 75). The ensuing swing to starboard brings the ship beam to wind. This is especially risky when we have to break out in light condition, as the wind has more grip on the light bow. To prevent the bow from being blown across, we leave the port anchor on the bottom, and we start heaving on the starboard chain. We may have to use the engine to break the port anchor out; with the port anchor on the bottom, we move the ship slowly over to where the starboard anchor is on the bottom, while heaving on the starboard chain (fig. 75, 3). Dredging the anchor has a stabilizing effect; when we stop the engine, the ship rapidly swings head to wind (fig. 75, 4).

There is the possibility of getting the port anchor in the starboard chain, but this can be safely cleared when the ship is heading out, head to wind.

Stern Anchor The stern anchor can be very useful either for anchoring in a strong current from aft, as for instance in the Mississippi River, or in combination with the bow anchor, when we can expect current from either fore or aft direction, as in tidal rivers. We need only glance at the force exerted by a current on the beam (page 64) to realize that a current from any other direction but fore and aft can have a disastrous effect. In estuaries, for instance, the direction of the tidal current may vary, which makes this type of anchoring, using bow as well as stern anchor, extremely hazardous. The difficulty encountered in dropping the stern anchor is that speed over the ground is not always easy to ascertain without a Doppler instrument. Ships are likely to keep some headway on, to be on the safe side, when the anchor is dropped. Good communication from bridge to fantail on letting go the anchor and slacking off the chain is important, especially when the bridge is amidships.

On picking up the stern anchor, there is the danger that the ship comes astern while heaving on the chain and that the anchor chain will foul the propeller. Masters with experience in using the stern anchor recommend keeping the bow anchor just on the bottom while heaving on the stern anchor, in order not to gather sternway and run the risk of fouling the propeller. Also, when the bow anchor is not used, it is a good idea to lower it on the bottom before starting to heave the stern anchor.

Emergency

In combination with the anchor, we can really knock the ship's speed down by swinging the ship at the same time. In case of an emergency, when we have to drop the anchor, we do well to start a swing to the side where we drop the anchor, provided, of course, that circumstances permit us to do so.

A loaded 47,000-dwt tanker under full speed managed to come to a stop within one mile by dropping the starboard anchor and slacking off the chain cautiously in such a way that it pulled the bow round to starboard. The emergency arose when the ship had a sudden blackout caused by generator trouble and was heading for the Maracaibo Bridge. (The bridge had recently reopened after it had been knocked over by a loaded tanker under similar circumstances.) The master rushed down from the bridge, amidships, to the fo'c'sle head. He had noticed that the ship had a slight swing to starboard which made him decide to drop the starboard anchor first, rather than drop both anchors at the same time. By cautiously and alternately checking and veering the chain, the starboard swing increased. Therefore, he did not' let go the port anchor, but thought of using it in case the chain of the starboard anchor broke. When the ship came at right angles to the original course, there were 8 shots of chain out, and the ship had come to a complete stop.

Even if stern power is available, a full turn takes less headroom than an emergency stop on full astern on the engine.

CHAPTER SEVEN

Narrow Channels

*Some men even with years of experience are
guilty of the mistake of relying or depending
too much on theory.*
    —Carlyle J. Plummer, *Ship Handling
    in Narrow Channels*

Wave making around the ship is increased
in shallow water due to the restriction in
the flow of water underneath the ship.
The wave profile alongside the ship shows
an increased wave ahead of the ship, a
deepened trough along the sides, and an
increased wave following the ship.

The increase in longitudinal resistance
causes a loss of speed. The deepened
trough makes the ship come closer to the
bottom (squat) and contributes to an increased restriction in water flow, and
again to a sharp reduction in speed. On
model tests it was found that sinkage is
directly proportional to the speed as well
as to the beam of the vessel.

An even greater flow restriction is encountered in narrow channels, where the
flow of water is restricted not only underneath the ship but also at the sides, resulting in Bernoulli pressure differences.

Bank Effect

A ship running close to a bank experiences
a significant drop in water level on the side
of the bank because of flow restriction. The
difference in water level at the ship's sides
causes a difference in pressure, which is
the source of a lateral force acting on the
ship in the direction of the bank (fig. 76).

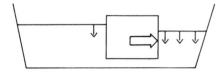

Fig. 76. Bernoulli effect: water flow restriction between ship and nearest bank results in increased flow rate and lower water level.

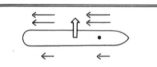

Fig. 77. Bank effect and pivot point.

The point of impact of the force is the center of gravity of the ship; the magnitude of the resulting transverse force acting on the center of gravity is directly proportionate to the difference in water level and is consequently directly related to the ship's speed.

The pivot point can be expected to be somewhere forward in the ship, which means that the effect of the transverse force acting on the center of gravity is to make the stern move toward the bank (fig. 77).

Moreover, when the ship is moving at a fairly high speed, there is a buildup of water at the bow, especially between the bow and the nearby bank, resulting in a difference in pressure on the onshore bow and the offshore bow. This is the source of a force which pushes the bow away from the bank.

A balance must be struck between the rudder force and the forces of bow cushion and stern suction in order to keep the ship steady near the bank. To keep the ship to one side of a canal, we have to keep rudder on; the closer to the bank the more rudder is needed to compensate for bank effect. As the effectiveness of the rudder is relatively higher in the region of smaller rudder angles, we not only limit our margin of rudder action, but we also eliminate that part which is most effective in steering the ship. The safest way to navigate narrow channels is to stay in the centerline when traffic allows us to do so.

Stern Suction and Pivot Point

When the ship is under the influence of bank effect and takes a sheer, the stern will come closer to the bank and suction, consequently, grows stronger (fig. 78). If we are late in taking action in breaking a sheer, we must overcome a much stronger force with increased leverage. Experience in taking a ship through narrow channels makes for anticipating suction and controlling it in time.

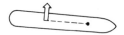

Fig. 78. Stern suction.

On a big tanker, we can expect strong suction effect in narrow channels because the wide beam causes extra sinkage, and the length of the large ship gives extra leverage to the suction. Furthermore, there is less room to break a developing sheer. By going slowly, we have more time to control weaker forces of bank effect, and, moreover, we have the possibility of increasing engine revolutions for extra steering control.

It can be seen that both suction and rudder force act as second-class levers, and that both forces gain in leverage when the pivot point moves forward.

An interesting situation arises when the tanker in figure 81 leaves East Channel by turning to starboard on full ahead and full right rudder. Suction draws the ship laterally to starboard and weakens the strength of the rudder force. The lateral force of the suction can be represented as a vector with its point of impact at G, leading to a situation similar to the one in figure 110, where the pivot point is abaft midships. The rudder acts in this case as a first-class lever in turning the bow to starboard, while the suction acts as a third-class lever. The stern of the tanker is held captive by the attraction to the reef due to suction, and the distance to the reef remains the same while the ship is turning out of the channel. Although the ship turns fast, the rate of turn is only half as much as the full turn of the same ship made at the same draft in deep water.

Bow Cushion and Pivot Point

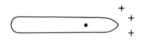

Fig. 79. Bow cushion.

The heightened bow wave increases the longitudinal resistance at the bow which tends to push the pivot point sternward. The buildup of water near the bank is higher than on the other bow resulting in a force exerted on the bow and pushing the bow away from the bank (fig. 79). The bow cushion has the same rotational direction as the stern suction, and its effect on deep draft ships with little bottom clearance can be strong.

However, owing to the position of the pivot point under forward motion of the ship, the bow cushion has less leverage than the stern suction. The bow cushion force depends upon the height of the bow wave which, in turn, varies with the bottom clearance, distance to the bank, and the ship's draft, beam, and speed.

We will experience bow cushion effect when we actually meet four conditions:

1. *Proximity to a bank.* Obviously, the bow wave will be more easily dispersed when the bank is submerged. Suction suffers to a lesser extent from loss in strength when the bank is submerged.

2. *The ship must be on a parallel course to the bank.* To build up the bow wave on the side of the bank, the ship must run parallel or close to parallel to the bank. Suction has a greater tolerance for the angle between ship and bank.

3. *The ship must reach a certain speed to build up a bow wave.* In this respect, the ship's speed is relative to its size, for we must take into account the ship's beam and bottom clearance as factors contributing to the height of the bow wave.

4. *The ship must have a large underwater area forward of the pivot point,* which is the case when the ship is in a loaded condition. Trim by the head increases the

88

underwater area forward of the pivot
point and, consequently, accentuates bow
cushion effect. In combination with point
3, we must take into account that the longitudinal component of the higher bow
wave in shallow water tends to push the
pivot point back, which will also increase
the lateral underwater area forward of
the pivot point, providing the transverse
component of the bow wave with added
leverage. Once a sheer sets in, the pivot
point tends to shift even farther back,
adding again to the force and the leverage
of the lateral resistance forward and
intensifying the sheer.

Most ships have a comparatively small
lateral underwater area forward of their
pivot point because of draft and trim. The
effect of the bow cushion is in that case insignificant and is at moderate speed not
noticeable.

When we handle a ship with a large
lateral underwater area forward of the
pivot point, we must avoid getting caught
in a situation where the bow cushion
starts a sheer, for that sheer is hard to
break! Given the right conditions, bow
cushion can be embarrassingly strong,
the more so since it is backed up followed
by an increasing effect of suction.

On a ship proceeding in a canal, the
bow cushion in itself is generally not very
bothersome, as it is either balanced by
equal pressure on both sides when the
ship is in the center of the canal, or coun-
terbalanced by a few degrees of rudder
when the ship is off-center. It is the drop
in pressure on one side that we have to
watch for, as it creates a sudden imbalance in forces on the foreship, which
starts a sheer. When, for instance, the
ship passes a branch canal, the buildup of
water on that side will disperse into the

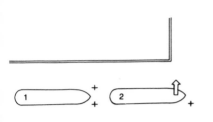

Fig. 80. Drop in bow wave
on one side.

branch canal (fig. 80, 2). At that moment the bow cushion on the other side becomes prominent and, if we are taken unawares, the ship will take a sheer.

Similarly, for a loaded tanker leaving San Nicolas, Aruba, there is a heightened bow wave on starboard, the buildup of water on the port bow being dissipated through a wide opening between the reef on that side. There is no noticeable bow cushion effect on tankers in ballast.

When the loaded tanker moves out slowly, not much rudder is required to control the tendency of the ship to swing to port, but it does need attention. If the effect of the bank rejection is not anticipated, it will be difficult to start a swing to starboard.

The stern suction comes a bit later on, when the starboard quarter passes close to the reef, with the accompanying tendency for the ship to swing to port, just as the time when the swing to starboard has to be set in to get the ship out to sea. If the initial tendency to swing to port was not anticipated and timely met, it will be very difficult to start the swing to starboard.

The bow cushion acts as a first-class lever. The objective of a first-class lever is the gain in speed rather than force; it is the speed of the effect of the bow cushion which can take us by surprise. The strength of the bow cushion force is dependent on the wave height and leverage. The danger is in the bow cushion gaining leverage, for if we are taken unawares, a strong bow cushion force will take the opportunity to turn itself into a second-class lever and shorten our steering lever. It is the reduction in steering leverage which may prevent us from developing an adequate response to overcome an even stronger bow cushion effect.

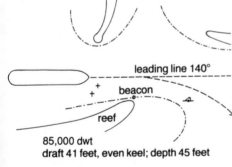

leading line 140°

beacon

reef

85,000 dwt
draft 41 feet, even keel; depth 45 feet

Fig. 81. Bow cushion effect
East Channel, Aruba.

90

When a big tanker in a loaded condition, trimmed by the head, is proceeding in the direction of East Channel (fig. 81), on the way out, we must be careful with the speed and be precise in steering. We are on the alert for the slightest turning motion to put preemptive rudder on; that is, more rudder than we would normally use. When full rudder is without visual effect, we must not hesitate in increasing engine revolutions to half or even full speed on the telegraph in order to prevent a sheer from developing.

The advantage of using full rudder is that the propeller thrust will be partly absorbed and partly deflected by the rudder, while longitudinal inertia slows acceleration of the ship. Suction and squat are both dependent on speed through the water, and it will take more time for the ship to pick up speed that it takes us to nip an incipient sheer in the bud.

When we see the ship straighten up under full rudder and increased engine speed, the first thing we do is to take the engine speed back to the original speed. Only then do we take off rudder partially, because as long as we are close to the bank, the ship is still under the influence of bank effect. We must keep some rudder on to counter this effect until the ship gets clear of the bank effect.

Restricted bottom clearance makes it unsafe for tankers to use the anchor. Huge oil spills have been caused by anchors piercing the ship's hull, which may be worse than a stranding. Otherwise, the use of anchors should not be overlooked.

How to drop an anchor for the purpose of breaking a sheer in order to avoid a collision with a ship that is being met is excellently described by Plummer in *Ship Handling in Narrow Channels*. There is a

Breaking a Sheer

91

lot of useful information in this book, the knowledge of shiphandling a "mud pilot" has which is also applicable to all ships of any size in shallow water.

Using Bank Effect to Advantage

Bank effect can be used to advantage when we have to swing the ship close to a bank and away from that bank, or when we have to navigate a bend in a narrow channel of a canal. Just before the bend we let the ship come off-center, so that we can control the bank effect by, say, 10 degrees of rudder. In the bend the ship will turn without rudder effort, that is, midships rudder, or a few degrees of rudder. Suction makes the ship turn, and we have all of the rudder available to control the swing. Suction steers the ship.

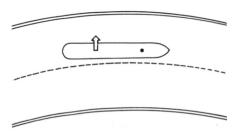

Fig. 82. Suction steers the ship.

Suction on Entering Port

We have the same helpful steering effect due to suction when we enter the port of San Nicolas, Aruba, and our ship has come over a bit to the north of the leading line. A swing to starboard is all right, for the loaded tankers have to go that way. Moreover, there is sufficient room to get rid of excessive speed before the ship arrives at the pier. If, however, for one reason or another, the ship comes in south of the leading line, we are in for trouble, especially when we have a good speed on.

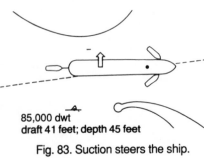

85,000 dwt
draft 41 feet; depth 45 feet

Fig. 83. Suction steers the ship.

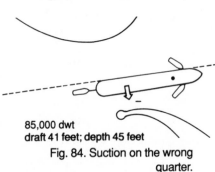

85,000 dwt
draft 41 feet; depth 45 feet

Fig. 84. Suction on the wrong quarter.

The stern passes close to the reef and suction on the starboard quarter causes the ship to sheer to port. It takes time before we straighten up with full ahead on hard right rudder, starboard tug backing full, port tug pushing full on the beam, and the tug right aft taking off the speed of the ship by backing. Starting a swing on a fully loaded ship takes time; it takes even more time to stop a swing because of the rotational momentum. It shows us how strong the suction is, that it can start a swing very quickly.

Meeting and Passing

When two ships must pass each other in a narrow channel, they should stay close to the middle of the channel or canal as long as possible. How close to each other they can approach before taking action depends on the situation, and on the maneuverability of the ships.

The thing to avoid is coming over to the side too soon and, due to bank effect, taking an uncontrollable sheer right across in front of the other ship. In restricted waterways this has often been the cause of collisions.

When the two ships pass each other in the right way, the effects are such that the two ships help each other by interaction. First their bow waves tend to push them apart and, when they have successfully passed each other, their stern suction will take their stern back to the center of the canal.

The passing procedure—and also how not to do it—has been described by Plummer in *Ship Handling in Narrow Channels*. With this in mind, at Grenoble, in the winter of 1967–68, I worked out a set of drawings, in figures 85 through 92, for use at the shiphandling training center, where we regularly practiced meeting and passing with scale models of tankers.

Fig. 85. Both ships have reduced engine revolutions; speed should be sufficient for good steering control. Both ships stay in the center as long as possible.

93

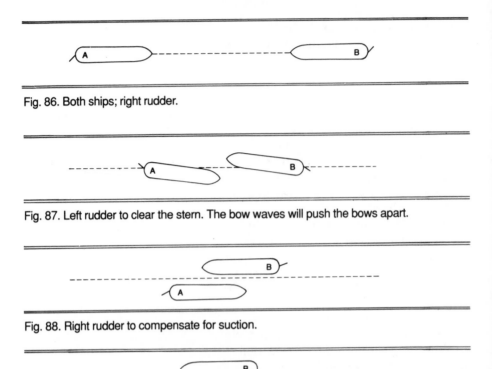

Fig. 86. Both ships; right rudder.

Fig. 87. Left rudder to clear the stern. The bow waves will push the bows apart.

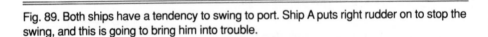

Fig. 88. Right rudder to compensate for suction.

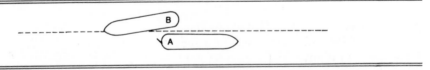

Fig. 89. Both ships have a tendency to swing to port. Ship A puts right rudder on to stop the swing, and this is going to bring him into trouble.

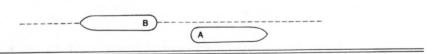

Fig. 90. A is now feeling the suction of B and has to put left rudder on to avoid the bank. The bow of B has come back to the center of the canal; now the stern will come back to the center by the suction of A.

Fig. 91. A has ended up too close to the bank and strongly feels the bank effect; B is back in the center of the canal and can increase speed for rudder control.

Fig. 92. Full right rudder could not stop the sheer caused by suction on ship A. Ship B used the interaction of the ships to advantage.

Overtaking

Overtaking in narrow channels is much more dangerous than passing. If it cannot be avoided, it should be done with reduced speeds only. The reason why it is so dangerous is that ships stay alongside each other much longer. Moreover, the effect on each other is anything but helpful, so that the only way to do it safely is to reduce the effects as much as possible by keeping the speed down. Figures 93 through 96 illustrate the procedure.

At the shiphandling training center at Port Revel, we often had disastrous but very instructive results when practicing overtaking in narrow channels. When working in scale models, the time factor is seldom felt as a disadvantage. On the contrary, more can be achieved within a limited period. Participants in the training course can gain a lot of shiphandling experience in a week's time. In fact, some claim that a week long course adds up to about two years of actual sea experience.

As I can remember, the final stage of the overtaking—when things happen so quickly and so adversely for the overtaken ship—is the only instance where we feel a bit hampered by the time factor. But then, the same time factor may be used as a face-saving excuse for running into difficulties. Nevertheless, the message about the danger of overtaking comes home.

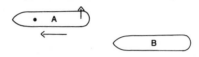

Fig. 93. At this stage the overtaken ship A already feels the effect of the overtaking ship B. The bow wave of B accelerates A, and at the same time pushes the stern over, an effect which will aggravate the effect of stern suction.

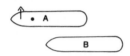

Fig. 94. At this stage A has a tendency to swing to starboard.

Fig. 95. The two bow waves push the bows apart, the mutual suction draws the sterns together, and, at the same time, A's speed reduces considerably. A is swinging toward the bank with a reduced speed and should not overreact, as that can bring him into trouble.

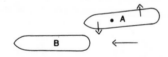

Fig. 96. The most dangerous stage where the overtaken ship is speeding up under the effect of the following wake of the overtaking ship. Suction at the stern of the overtaking ship and suction at the stern near the bank form a strong turning couple. Often A is irresistibly drawn toward the stern of B. The overtaking ship does not feel much effect of the overtaken ship. It is mainly bank effect that the overtaking ship must cope with.

A master of a tanker, who was a graduate of the shiphandling training course at Grenoble, told me later in Ras Tanura that he was about to overtake a tanker in the approach channel leading to Ras Tanura. On second thought, however, he decided not to overtake as he remembered what could happen.

96

Practical Applications

*Toute manoeuvre est une anticipation con-
stante. Ce qui distingue la manoeuvre d'un
bateau de celle d'un navire, c'est que l'on fait
par habitude et presque sans y penser sur les
premiers ce qui, sur les derniers, demande
de la réflexion et des précautions. L'échelle
seule varie.*
    —Pierre Célérier, *La Manoeuvre des
    Navires*

We will discuss the handling of tankers,
varying in size from 25,000 to 250,000-
dwt , assisted by screw-propelled tugs. All
ships under consideration have a single
right-handed propeller. Scale models are
fitted out with a bow thruster, some with
a stern thruster as well. The effect
of tug and bow thruster is not always the
same; the difference has been discussed
in chapter 4.

When similar maneuvers, as the ones
discussed in this chapter, are attempted
with scale models, a conscious effort should
be made to use the thruster as if it were a
tug. On docking, we can still use the thruster when the model is alongside, whereas
on the real ship we must stop the thruster
for line handling.

*Loaded, with the aid of a single tug made
fast at ⅓ length.*

Case 1. Undocking a 25,000-dwt Tanker

We order the tug to pull, and we come
ahead on the engine on hard left rudder to
lift the stern off (fig. 97, 1). the ship now
moves laterally away from the dock, but
when head motion sets in, the pivot point

97

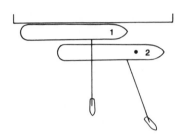

Fig. 97. Single tug, made fast at ⅓ length.

Fig. 98. Alternative use of single tug.

moves forward, and we must put the rudder back to midships, otherwise the ship starts swinging to port. The tug seems to have little effect as the loaded tanker meets a lot of lateral resistance. After we order the tug to come to the left, in order not to override the tug, there is even less lateral effect (fig. 97, 2).

As long as the stern will not clear the dock we cannot start a swing to starboard by using the rudder. When we want the ship to swing to starboard, we stop all forward motion by coming astern on the engine. When the forward motion of the ship comes off, the pivot point moves back, and the tug will have sufficient leverage to pull the bow to starboard.

The tug would have had greater leverage had it been pulling at the bow. Rudder and engine could then be used to keep the ship parallel while leaving the berth and in this way add to the power of the single tug in obtaining lateral motion. In figure 98, we consider two situations:

Assisted ship A should not come ahead. We hold on to a long back spring forward, taking care not to put a shock load on it. The tug pulls in a direction abaft the beam, and we come ahead on hard left rudder. As soon as the bow comes clear of the vessel ahead of us we stop the engine and let go the spring.

Assisted ship B sails from pier end; there is no room to come astern. The tug is best positioned as far forward as possible, preferably pushing on the inshore bow. The stern can be lifted off by rudder plus engine, which adds to the power of the single tug. Backspring from main deck is last line to let go.

The advantage of a tug pushing is that we do not depend on the breaking strength of the towing rope. In swell condition, however, the tug is better on the line in order not to damage the tug's fenders.

Note: There is a noticeable difference in effect between a dock that has a solid wall and a ·dock built on a pile structure. When there is a solid wall the stern will be drawn in under head motion because of suction.

In ballast, stern first into an offshore wind.

The combined effect of the transverse thrust of the propeller and the 25-knot wind on the starboard quarter keeps the stern out. In order to get the stern in we increase the force of the after tug. Instead of canting the stern in, we see that as a result of the increased push of the after tug, the ship moves bodily in without a noticeable swing.

The turning effect of the after tug is zero, as the point of impact is too close to the pivot point. To get the stern in we must back the forward tug which has effective leverage at this stage. All the steering must be done with the forward tug; the rudder and the after tug have little or no steering effect as long as the ship is under sternway. As the after tug gives only lateral motion while the ship is backing, we can let it push all the time to compensate for the offshore wind effect. Against a combination of a strong wind and tide we need a strong tug aft.

Once the sternway comes off, the effect of the tugs will be different with the shift in position of the pivot point. Another consideration that we have to keep in mind is that we must keep the tugs in a good position, that is, at right angles to the ship. By having the tugs completely stopped, they may fall flat alongside, except for the forward tug, while the ship is backing. A line from the stern of the tug to the ship prevents the tug from falling across the bow.

Case 2. Docking a 36,000-dwt Tanker

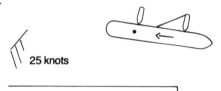

25 knots

Fig. 99. Docking stern first in off-shore wind.

99

Flanking rudders improve the performance of screw-propelled tugs by allowing them to keep position when their engine is working astern. Twin-screw tugs can keep position by reversing one engine, but by doing so lose out on output. The Voight-Schneider type of tugs and tugs with steerable rudder propellers, as Schottel tugs and Z-drive tugs, seem to have no problem in keeping position.

Case 3. Docking a 50,000-dwt Tanker

22 knots

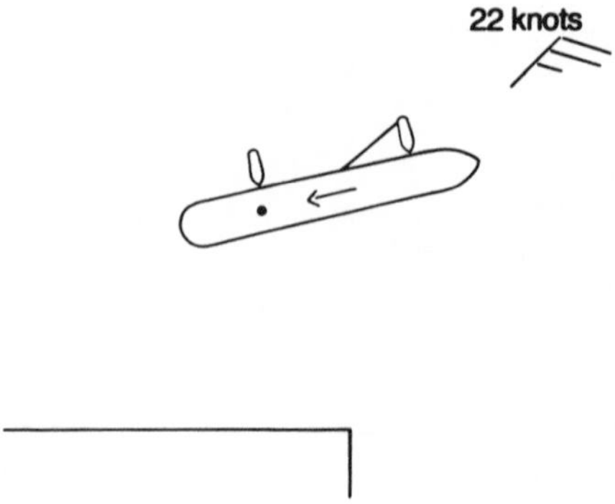

Fig. 100. Docking stern first, in an onshore wind.

In ballast, stern first, wind on offshore bow.

We must be careful not to give the wind a grip on the bow at the time when the ship has sternway and the pivot point is aft. The transverse wind-force has then powerful leverage and its moment increases rapidly with a swing of the ship to starboard. In order to minimize the magnitude of the transverse wind-force we keep the bow angled out as much as possible. For this reason we must start out on this maneuver well to windward to allow ourselves sufficient leeway (fig. 100).

Tidal conditions can play a pivotal role. Coming down with the tide the ship is more manageable, hardly or not at all moving through the water. Coming astern against the tide at a good speed through the water in order to obtain relative motion, the ship is more difficult to control, as the pivot point remains aft for a long period of time.

The bow is to be kept under control by backing the forward tug most of the time. If the bow comes over a bit too far to starboard and the forward tug loses out to the transverse wind-force, we can come ahead on full left rudder. We not only decrease the magnitude of the transverse wind-force by diminishing the angle between bow and wind, but we also shorten the lever of the transverse wind-force at the same time by taking off sternway. The combination enables us to regain control. However, once a good swing to starboard is on, it is almost impossible to stop the swing without parting the tug's lines. If this happens, we must drop the port anchor to check the bow from falling across.

The force to starboard and the ensuing rotational motion is notably increased when a larger part of the windage is forward, as is the case with a ship that is very much down by the stern or with a ship that has the midship house well forward. The bridge aft brings the windage more aft and in this respect facilitates this type of docking.

Apart from such considerations as stern power, tide, and trim, the bridge position may very well be the determining factor in our decision to take the ship in or not, in cases where the wind has reached the maximum allowable velocity for safe berthing.

If the assisting tugs are not equal in power, we take the stronger tug forward. As long as the ship has sternway and the pivot point is aft, we keep the bow out to reduce the strain on the lines of the forward tug.

Under marginal conditions, the right-handed propeller has a definite advantage in starboard side-to dockings as it helps to keep the stern up, where a left-handed propeller, working astern, makes it necessary to keep the bow a bit more to leeward in order to keep the stern up. Not until the ship reaches the right position in relation to the dock do we allow the bow to come in. By then the ship has lost sternway, the pivot point has moved forward, and the decrease in leverage of the transverse wind-force makes it easier to control the bow.

A forward motion in the final stage of docking further reduces the leverage of the transverse wind-force. However, this forward motion may get the tugs out of position, unless we can allow the tugs to push very easy and remain in good position for backing on the beam.

Case 4. Undocking a 70,000-dwt Tanker

Loaded, with the assistance of two tugs, current from aft.

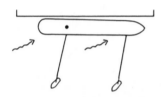

Fig. 101. Undocking in current from aft.

The ship is moving through the water and is, in fact, making sternway as long as the ship remains in position relative to the dock. In order to prevent the ship from coming ahead, we let go the forward back spring last. The tugs are heading up current (fig. 101).

The after tug seems to have little effect as it pulls close to the pivot point. It is difficult to start lateral motion away from the dock; the transverse component of the current, which strikes the ship on the starboard quarter, pushes the stern in. In contrast, the merest strain on the line of the forward tug is sufficient to bring the bow out, and the ensuing swing to starboard exposes an increasing target to the current.

Taking into consideration the enormous strength of a current on the beam, specifically in cases where there is little bottom clearance, it is obvious that taking the ship out in this way is extremely risky even in a weak current, let alone in a strong current. The best we can do under the circumstances is to give the ship forward motion as soon as possible. We must be careful not to override the tugs and order them to come to the left. With forward motion of the ship, the pivot point will come forward, increasing the leverage of the after tug. The after tug would be in a

102

better position to start with had it been made fast right aft.

The only safe way to take the ship out in a current from aft with a ship ahead of us is to pull the stern off first (fig. 102). We hold on to the forward backspring and let the after tug pull first. The transverse force of the current decreases while the stern comes off until the current comes right from aft. The safest way for unberthing a loaded tanker in an unfavorable current is always to bring the ship parallel with the current as soon as possible. Any more swing at this moment will bring the current on the port quarter and the transverse current force will take the ship off. Backing the ship out keeps the pivot point aft and makes it easy enough for the forward tug to pull the bow off.

When the current is very strong and a third tug is available, we put this extra tug aft on the main deck, to keep clear of the tug right aft. Bigger ships require more bollard pull, and we put the stronger tug on that side of the ship where the current comes in on the ship. On a loaded VLCC in a strong tide from aft we try to slip an extra tug in to push on the port quarter as soon as the two after tugs have pulled the stern sufficiently out to allow that tug to come in between ship and dock. However, we do this only when there is no ship ahead of us, otherwise it is safer to wait until the tide changes. The forward tug cannot even put a strain on the line as this tends to pull the bow out too early.

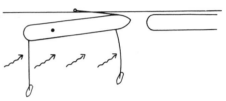

Fig. 102. Diminishing the angle under which the current strikes the quarter.

Loaded, backing out; no wind, no tide, bottom clearance 40 feet.

Case 5. Undocking a 100,000-dwt Tanker

Two tugs are on the line, pulling the ship off on half power (fig. 103, 1). Because the ship has to back out, both tugs

103

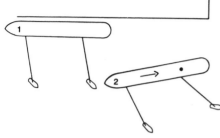

Fig. 103. Backing out.

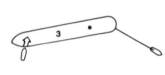

Fig. 104. Turning under sternway.

are heading in a direction abaft the beam, which gives the ship sternway. As the bow starts swinging to port, we must slow down the forward tug. The after tug pulls close to the center of lateral resistance and the pivot point and has zero leverage. After starting the engine on astern we must stop the forward tug altogether. We give left rudder, either full or 20 degrees.

The transverse thrust of the propeller working astern is having no noticeable effect; neither has the rudder (fig. 103, 2). The ship is moving astern at a speed of about 1 knot.

A strain on the line of the forward tug is sufficient to bring the bow out; for that reason we let go the forward tug. We come full ahead on hard right rudder to stop the swing to port: it takes time to stop the swing because of the rotational momentum of the loaded ship and the small rudder leverage under sternway. We stop the engine when we have stopped the swing to port. Sternway is still on because of the ship's longitudinal momentum.

The after tug is still pulling on half power (fig. 104, 3). We have the after tug made fast where it should have been in the first place—right aft. Still, the tug is obviously pulling close to the pivot point and is lacking leverage. The forward tug starts pushing the bow round to starboard.

Case 6. Docking a 140,000-dwt Tanker

In ballast, between ships; wind and tide from opposite directions.

We choose to make our approach heading into the stronger force. The ballasted ship is affected more by the strong wind than by the weak tide. When wind and current are not from exactly opposite directions, there will be a transverse force of either of them. We must assess their effect on the ship and decide which of the two we will try to eliminate as much as possible in the approach.

As the tide is not strong we decide to come in heading into the 20-knot wind which is parallel to the dock. The current runs at an angle of about 10 degrees to the dock (fig. 105).

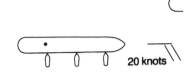

Fig. 105. Parallel with the wind.

When stopped relative to the dock, the ship is making sternway through the water on account of the current, and the pivot point will consequently be aft. There will be a transverse component of the current force when the ship is parallel to the dock. As we are heading straight into the wind, we have no transverse wind-force to cope with.

To keep the ship stopped relative to the dock, we must come astern on the engine, and the transverse thrust of the propeller may start a cant. The after tug has its point of impact near the pivot point and has zero leverage. If the after tug cannot prevent the stern from coming in, a much larger part of the ship's underwater starboard side will be exposed to current.

It can be seen that the ship can get into a dangerous position when a starboard swing sets in. We will therefore examine what will happen when we have the stern farther out during the approach.

Fig. 106. Parallel with the current.

With the current right aft, there will be no transverse current force, but now we have a constant transverse wind-force to cope with (fig. 106).

Our main problem is to prevent the forward tug from falling alongside as we need the tug for backing to keep the bow up. The safest way for berthing is to keep the ship parallel with the current as long as possible. It is always good practice to take off entirely the lateral motion some way off the dock and then to start moving in again, particularly when the approach is not parallel with the dock. An underestimation of the lateral momentum will result in a one-point landing when we are not able to check the lateral motion in time.

When the current is very strong, we better make the approach heading into the current, specifically with a loaded or partly loaded ship. The head current will allow us to use engine and rudder when the longitudinal current force is stronger than the longitudinal wind-force.

The rudder force is most effective as long as the ship is moving ahead through the water, and the pivot point is forward. However, in this case the transverse wind-force has effective leverage as well and keeps bothering us during the approach. Once the ship comes into position relative to the dock and all speed is off, the tugs can better position themselves and balance the transverse force of the wind.

If the ship is to move in the very last stage of docking, it is better to move with the current than against the current. Moving against the current may bring the tugs, when they are pulling, flat alongside. Moreover, the pivot point moves away from amidships. The tug close to the pivot point will have insufficient leverage to check the lateral motion caused by the transverse current force at the moment when the ship comes parallel with the dock and the ship's side becomes exposed to the current to a greater degree. Thus it is good practice in a head current to come, 20 to 40 feet or so, ahead of the final position before arriving at the very last stage of berthing and to let the ship drift back in. In a following current we leave some room ahead of us to let the ship into during the very last stage of berthing (Appendix A, 2).

In ballast, with the assistance of three tugs, 4,000 HP each.

The ship is proceeding at a speed of about one knot. We put the engine slow astern to take the speed off. Meanwhile, we let the three tugs push very easy to start moving the ship in and to get the tugs in a good position.

If we expect the ship to swing to starboard because of the transverse thrust of the propeller, we are in for a surprise. The ship swings to port. As the ship is moving ahead through the water, the pivot point is still forward and this gives the after tug very effective leverage. For this reason we must watch closely in which direction the ship is moving through the water, and we must regulate the force of the tugs and balance other forces acting on the ship. A wind on the port quarter, for instance, has the same effect in swinging the ship to port when the ship is under forward motion through the water.

Current complicates matters insofar as the ship can be moving through the water when there is no motion relative to the dock. The pivot point moves from the midship in the direction the ship moves through the water.

When we handle a turbine tanker, and the current is from aft, it is a good practice to leave some engine revolutions on astern when the ship is almost in position relative to the dock. The reason for this is that the engine room may give us some revolutions ahead which, on some ships, take quite some time to reverse. The current may meanwhile have given the ship a good forward motion. In a strong onshore beam wind, it is hazardous to move the ship back to recover the distance lost due to the response lapse. The increased leverage of the wind-force may trip the

Case 7. Docking a 190,000-dwt Tanker

Fig. 107. Pivotal considerations.

balance when the pivot point has moved too far aft. In this case the middle tug would be in a better position farther forward, closer to the first tug.

However, not all ships offer a choice of chocks, and we either have to make the best of a bad arrangement or decline docking a ship because the safety margin is too slim. The force exerted on the bow by wave action must be taken into account in our decision, as this may add an extra 10 to 20 tons in workable condition.

A Doppler is very helpful in giving us information on the lateral speed. Particularly in the situation just described where the reading on the instrument tells us whether we can control the side motion or not when we back the tugs some safe distance off the berth.

In nice weather it may seem easy enough to get the ship alongside once the ship is stopped some distance off and parallel to the dock. However, it requires constant observation, evaluation, anticipation, and concentration to take the ship alongside without causing an impact load.

We must observe the ship's position in relation to the dock to judge the relative speed. We observe flags or smoke from the funnel to determine the wind direction, and we may check the wind speed recorder occasionally. We observe the tugs to see if they are in a good position. We observe rudder angle, engine revolutions, longitudinal and lateral speed by keeping an eye on rudder indicator, RPM indicator, and Doppler. We observe the angle of approach by checking the repeater compass. We evaluate the forces that affect the ship and try to anticipate different effects with a change in ship's speed and direction. We concentrate on the various orders we give to the tugs, to the person at the telegraph and to the person on the wheel, while contacting the spotter on the dock for information on the position of the ship's manifold in relation to the shore connection, and, if the ship has short bridgewings, on the distance between ship and shore when the mooring dolphins are lost sight of in the last stage of docking. Meanwhile, we may have all kinds of dialogue going on the same frequency that we use for our contact with the tugs and the spotter at the shore manifold. The excess steam may at this moment choose to burst from the funnel, and things on board may not exactly go the way we would have liked, or the way we have instructed.

In practice, inefficiency and deficiencies usually pose more of a problem than the actual shiphandling itself. Shipboard communications, for instance, often leave much to be desired. The few indicators there are, such as revolution counter, rudder indicator, and Doppler, are not seldom out of order. The hands on deck on board tankers are often inexperienced and too few in number. Shiphandling requires the ability to adjust, to compensate, to allow for, and, quite often, to make do.

In any case, no matter what size or shape the ship, shiphandling remains a pivotal operation. This knowledge helps us in the process of balancing the forces and in preventing excessive dynamic loads.

Case 8. Undocking a 250,000-dwt Tanker

Loaded with the assistance of three tugs, 4,000 HP each; subsequently, turning the ship to starboard; slack water; Doppler speed indicator.

The three tugs have given the ship a lateral speed of 0.30 knots. We let go the tugs and come ahead half on hard right rudder (35 degrees). It takes quite a while

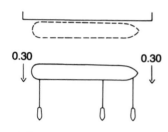

Fig. 108. Lateral motion.

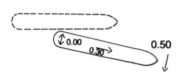

Fig. 109. Using engine and rudder while the ship is under lateral motion.

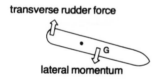

Fig. 110. Lateral momentum.

before the ship starts swinging and moving ahead. We read the Doppler and see that the motion of the stern decreases slowly to zero lateral speed. The lateral speed of the bow has meanwhile increased from 0.30 to 0.50 knots, when at this time the forward motion of the ship has come up to a speed of 0.30 knots (fig. 109).

Where is the pivot point?

Since the ship is making headway (0.3 knots), we would expect the pivot point to be forward. Half ahead on hard right rudder would also mean that the pivot point should be well forward. However, the Doppler gives zero lateral speed aft and 0.50 knots lateral speed of the bow to starboard, suggesting a rotation about the stern.

The readings of the Doppler give us a momentary picture of what seems to be simple swing, but which is, in fact, a combination of three motions which are going on at this time—lateral motion stemming from lateral momentum, longitudinal motion generated by the propulsion force, and rotational motion induced by the rudder force. The impetus for the increase in lateral motion of the foreship is the leverage of the center of gravity which developed when rotational motion set in. Part of the lateral speed of the foreship is generated rotational motion, part is original lateral momentum. The lateral speed of the aft ship has at this time come down to zero, which means that the rotational motion generated by the rudder force has nullified the lateral motion of the stern. Next moment, however, the lateral speed of the aft ship will show up again, but now as lateral motion to port.

The pivot point is between the center of gravity and the rudder (fig. 110), closer to amidships than to the stern, as the lateral

110

speed of the foreship has come up less
(0.20 knots) than the lateral speed aft has
come down (0.30 knots).

It is an indication of the magnitude of
the lateral momentum that it has kept
the pivot point back for so long while the
ship has built up longitudinal speed to 0.3
knots. With a further waning of the lateral momentum, the pivot point moves forward, increasing the leverage of the
rudder force.

As long as the lateral speed of the stern
to port is not at least twice the lateral
speed of the bow to starboard, there is
still lateral momentum on. The length of
time it takes the lateral momentum to
wear itself out is a measure of its strength.

When we continue the swing to starboard, we see that the longitudinal speed
comes up to 3.00 knots (fig. 111). The
stern has a lateral speed to port of 1.20
knots, and the bow a lateral speed to starboard of 0.20 knots, resulting in a net lateral motion to port.

In a current, the readings on the Doppler need to be interpreted, taking into account the direction the ship moves in the
current. For instance, when there is a
head current of 0.5 knots while the ship is
still tied up alongside and, in fact, moving
through the water at a speed of 0.5 knots,
this speed does not show up when the Doppler gives the speed over the ground.

On letting go the lines the ship has a
longitudinal momentum in the direction
against the current. After making a 90-
degree turn to the right, the momentum
will show up as longitudinal motion.
When the current is on the beam, it will
move the ship sideways at a speed of 0.5
knots. A swing of the bow to starboard of
0.20 knots now reads as 0.70 knots to star-

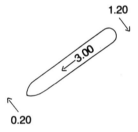

Fig. 111. Doppler readings on
rudder force.

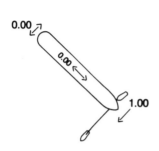

Fig. 112. Utilizing leverage.

board, and 1.20 knots lateral speed of the stern to port now shows up as 0.70 knots to port. Not taking the current into account, we would conclude from the readings that the ship was pivoting about midships.

For a tighter swing to starboard we can let the forward tug continue pulling on the line while letting go the other tugs. If now we come ahead on full right rudder, we reduce the leverage of the tug because of resultant headway and forwarding of the pivot point. Moreover, instead of net lateral motion to starboard, we may still have a net lateral motion to port which, together with increasing head motion, widens the turn.

Instead of coming ahead on hard right rudder, we let one of the two released tugs come and push on the port bow to reinforce the leverage of the forward tug and thus expedite the job (fig. 112).

By coming astern on the engine and by taking off all head motion, we give the tugs as much leverage as possible. With a reading of a constant zero longitudinal speed and a constant zero lateral speed of the stern, we read 1.00 knot lateral speed of the bow to starboard, indicating that the ship pivots about the stern.

A faster rate of turn can be achieved by having the second tug push on the starboard quarter or pull on the port quarter. However, the bow is a better place to push, allowing the tug to come close to the end of the ship. Making fast with a line aft is not so attractive for reasons of expediency.

The disadvantage of using the rudder for turning is that only part of the propulsion force is converted into rudder force. Some ships can give 45 degrees of rudder which gives a faster rate of turn at a relatively lower acceleration of longitudinal speed. It is very helpful in making a tight swing within the limitations of its use (speed under 8 knots, RPM under 50).

Doppler Readings

The Doppler gives us helpful information. The numerical values given in the text are not to be taken too seriously. It should be realized that some of the readings are of a very low order and that the figures jump and change all the time during the maneuver. A correction on the reading of the lateral motion should, in fact, be applied when the transducers are not located at the very end of the ship. Anyway, the readings give us an overall picture of the maneuver, and by interpreting these readings I have tried to explain the underlying principles of shiphandling.

I have drawn my conclusions from my own observations. Ships fitted out with a reliable docking Doppler in the bridge-wing are still few and far between. My observations were not always made under ideal conditions. Moreover, there was first and foremost the maneuver to consider, which did not always allow me to give my undivided attention to reading the Doppler. The figures used in the text are believed to be correct. They fit the pattern of ship behavior that I have explained in the foregoing chapters.

Shiphandling Theory

Shiphandling theory has never been held in high regard because, in practice, it failed to explain ship behavior under all circumstances. The major flaw in the theory is that the turning lever of a force acting on the ship was considered with respect to the center of gravity of the ship.

Shiphandling hinges on the pivot point. The pivot point is the hub of all rotational motion. Its position depends upon the interaction among the several forces acting on the ship.

Underwater resistance has a marked effect on the pivot point, but it was not taken into account as a force in shiphandling theory. Another important force, which was not fully recognized in shiphandling theory, was the ship's mass. The center of gravity itself has leverage with respect to the pivot point and can be the point of impact of a rotational force when the ship's mass manifests itself as momentum.

Handling Big Ships

From a shiphandling point of view, handling the big tankers is, in principle, not much different from handling the smaller ships, provided of course that sufficient tug horsepower is available. The main difference is the difference in momentum. The momentum of the big one is tremendous, whereas its horsepower is comparatively low.

To prevent excessive dynamic loads on lines of ships and tugs, speed—longitudinal, lateral as well as rotational—should be kept at a minimum. By making a careful approach, the ship is subjected to wind and current for a longer period of time. Since exposed broadside area is so much larger, the forces of wind and current are so much greater. Consequently, our safety margin must be wider. A wind-force that may not deter us from berthing a 25,000 tonner makes us think twice before taking in a 250,000 tonner.

Angle of Approach

All these considerations lead up to a difference in approach—the bigger the ship the more the longitudinal approach makes way for the lateral approach. As any impact load on contact must be spread over as wide as possible an area, one-point landings must be avoided.

Another difference is the time factor—things happen very slowly on the big ones. When we are waiting for a response, it

114

can be exasperatingly slow. We must
think and plan well in advance and set in
a maneuver sooner than we would do on a
small tanker. We must try and prevent
getting into a situation where we have to
take forceful measures—on the big ones
patience will, in most cases, achieve more
than force.

Lateral Motion

1. Lateral Resistance

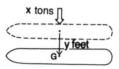

Fig. 113. Transverse force on ship on even keel, dead in the water.

Under the effect of a transverse force the ship starts moving sideways through the water after inertia has been overcome. The ship displaces water and experiences drag set up by underwater resistance. The lateral resistance depends upon the lateral underwater area: a deeper draft gives a greater underwater area and greater resistance; a different trim affects the relative resistance forward and aft, causing the center of lateral resistance to be either forward or aft of amidships, leading to rotational motion under midships transverse pressure. Let us consider a ship on even keel affected by a transverse force amidships (fig. 113). The point of impact of the transverse force coincides with the center of gravity as well as with the center of lateral resistance. The useful effect of a force of x tons displacing the center of gravity y feet is xy feet/tons. The single force amidship can be replaced, with the same effect, by two forces equidistant from midships each half the strength of the single force.

2. Effect of Longitudinal Motion

When the ship is under longitudinal motion through the water, the point of impact of the transverse force amidships no longer coincides with the center of lateral resistance. The center of lateral resistance is somewhere forward under forward motion of the ship and will serve as a soft fulcrum for rotational motion. The center for the rotational motion will be the pivot

point, which is near the center of lateral
resistance and is at y feet from the point
of impact of the transverse force of x tons;
the lever for rotational motion will be xy
ft/tons. Under stern motion, the center of
lateral resistance will be aft, and the lever
will again by xy ft/tons (fig. 114).

On docking a vessel with the aid of tugs
pushing alongside, the lateral motion of
the ship must be maintained up to the moment of contact of the ship with the mooring dolphins. It is easier to maintain a
balance of transverse forces when the ship
is not under longitudinal motion through
the water. This means that in a head current, we let the ship drift back in, relative
to the dock; in a current from aft we let
the ship move ahead with the speed of the
current in the final stage of docking.

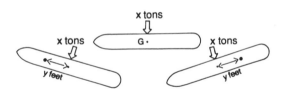

Fig. 114. Transverse force on ship under longitudinal motion.

Two transverse forces of x tons equidistant from amidships; ship is not under longitudinal motion (fig. 115). Center of
gravity and center of lateral resistance coincide. Lateral effect: 2 x tons.

The vectors represent forces exerted by
tugs, thrusters, or propeller/rudder combination. When the tugs are working on the
hook, their lines can be made fast at the
far ends of the assisted ship; when working alongside, the tugs can occasionally
come and push at the bow or stern of the

3. Long Levers

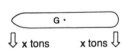

Fig. 115. Long levers: no longitudinal motion.

117

assisted ship if that vessel is in loaded condition. If the assisted ship is in light condition, the flare of the bow or the counter may not allow the tug to work there.

4. Long Levers under Longitudinal Motion

Ship moving ahead through the water; can be stationary relative to the dock in a head current (fig. 116). In order to keep the ship parallel to the dock, the after tug is using less power than the forward tug, let us say for the sake of convenience: ½x tons.

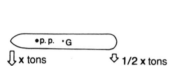

Fig. 116. Long levers; ship under longitudinal motion.

In figure 98, where the transverse forces are made up by forward tug and resulting transverse force of propeller thrust on full rudder, we should not develop much headway, as this would result in reduced leverage for the forward tug.

5. Short Levers

The transverse forces of x ton exerted equidistant from amidships; ship dead in the water (fig. 117). Center of gravity and center of lateral resistance coincide. Lateral effect: 2x tons.

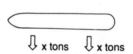

Fig. 117. Short levers; no longitudinal motion.

Tugs working alongside are at a safe distance from bow and stern. Occasionally, a ship has no chocks on the maindeck to make fast the tugs, because the ship was built to trade between ports where tugs on the hook are employed.

6. Short Levers under Longitudinal Motion

Ship moving ahead through the water; point of impact of forward tug and pivot point coincide (fig. 118). In order to keep the ship parallel to the dock, the after tug has to be stopped altogether and should not put a strain on the line. Lateral effect: x tons.

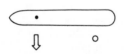

Fig. 118. Short levers; ship under headway.

In figure 103, both tugs are made fast on the main deck. As long as the assisted ship is not under longitudinal motion, the performance of the tugs in pulling the ves-

118

sel off laterally is not affected by their leverage. Under stern motion of the assisted ship, rotational motion sets in, which makes it seem that the tug aft is performing poorly. If we are not satisfied with the tug's performance, it is not the tug that is at fault. Not only has the tug zero leverage, but also its angle of effort is not optimal, because the tug has to adjust to the direction of motion of the assisted ship.

The forward tug (fig. 103) still seems to pull and to ignore our order to stop. In practice, the tug often has to put a strain on its line to maintain position. For that reason, we should release the forward tug as soon as possible.

The ship is moving ahead through the water; the transverse forces of forward tug and middle tug are equal and are exerted equidistant from the pivot point. We must stop the after tug; otherwise it upsets the balance (fig. 119). Lateral effect: 2x tons. If the middle tug had been made fast closer to the pivot point, the after tug could have augmented the total transverse force.

Under head motion of the assisted ship, the forward tug has most leverage when its line is made fast as far forward as possible. When the tugs are working on the hook, there is usually no problem in finding chocks in the right place for the two tugs forward. However, if the tugs are working alongside, we may experience difficulties in finding proper chocks.

Not all ships—including VLCCs—offer a wide choice of chocks. Occasionally, we may have to accept a crossbitt near the manifold to take the line of the middle tug; in that case we must keep in mind

7. Effect of Tugs under Headway

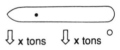

Fig. 119. Three tugs pulling or pushing on the beam: ship is moving ahead through the water.

8. Effect of Tugs under Sternway

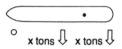

Fig. 120. Ship moving astern: three tugs push or pull on the beam.

not to exceed the maximum safe bollard pull.

The ship is moving astern through the water; the transverse forces of middle tug and after tug are exerted equidistant from the pivot point (fig. 120). The forward tug should not put a strain on the line unless the middle tug is made fast closer to the pivot point. Lateral effect: 2x tons.

Under stern motion of the assisted ship, the after tug has most leverage when its line is made fast as far aft as possible (as shown in figure 104). When we take out a loaded VLCC as described in chapter 8, case 4, in a current striking the quarter, we use maximum available horsepower at optimal leverage to lift the stern off. The desired lateral motion can safely be set in when the current comes in from right aft, which means that the assisted ship is parallel with the current.

Rotational Motion

A ship under speed—on a certain trim and draft—will meet lateral resistance under rudder effect. The center of lateral resistance serves the rudder as a soft fulcrum for the swing. The ship rotates about the pivot point which is near the center of lateral resistance. As the drift angle opens up under the swing, lateral resistance also develops against the exposed ship's side. Whereas the rudder force depends upon rudder angle and propeller thrust, lateral resistance depends upon drift angle and speed through the water. A deeper draft increases the lateral underwater area and consequently the lateral resistance; a different trim alters the relative area forward and aft of the pivot point.

FR (lateral resistance forward of the pivot point) (fig. 121) has a direct rotational effect and is one of the principal forces which determines the position of the pivot point on a ship turning under rudder. The center of the FR (R′) is located about halfway between the bow and the pivot point.

AR (lateral resistance which acts abaft the pivot point) is working against the rudder force and has as such only an indirect effect on the turn inasmuch as it restricts the drift angle. The drift angle opens up until the AR has reached a certain proportion of the transverse rudder force. This proportion is sooner reached in shallow water where restricted bottom clearance causes a buildup of water on the

1. Lateral Resistance

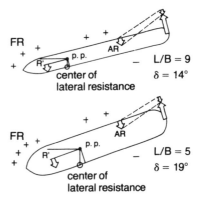

Fig. 121. Lateral resistance abaft the pivot point restricts the drift angle.

side to which the stern moves. The resulting smaller drift angle leads to a wider turn.

On a ship under speed, the initial pivot point under rudder effect is about halfway between the bow and the center of gravity, that is, at the very outset of the turn when both drift angle and lateral resistance are minimal. Not only is there a relatively larger lateral underwater area abaft the initial pivot point, but also the speed through the water is, as yet, unaffected, which makes for a strong initial AR. Therefore, the drift angle opens up slowly as the transverse rudder force has to overcome lateral inertia as well as strong AR, resulting in an initial low rate of turn for the first 10 degrees of turn. A widening drift angle causes a growing FR to push the pivot point back until the maximum drift angle has been reached, at which time the AR limits the rudder force, and a competitive balance will be established between lateral resistance and rudder force.

Beamy ships and ships down by the head meet stronger FR. Consequently, the lateral underwater area abaft the pivot point will be smaller and the drift angle must open up farther to bring the AR up to a certain proportion of the transverse rudder force (fig. 121).

The rate of turn is highest at the time of the higher resistance at the bow, not long after the turn has well set in, that is, between 10 and 90 degrees of turn. In a later stage of the full turn, when the speed has come down to a constant speed and the engine revolutions are higher than consistent with the speed through the water, the pivot point has moved forward again, resulting in a lower rate of turn.

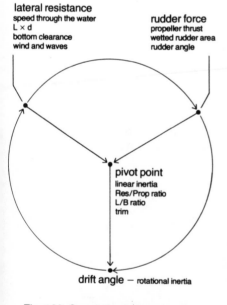

lateral resistance
speed through the water
L × d
bottom clearance
wind and waves

rudder force
propeller thrust
wetted rudder area
rudder angle

pivot point
linear inertia
Res/Prop ratio
L/B ratio
trim

drift angle — rotational inertia

Fig. 122. Correlation between rudder force, drift angle, lateral resistance, and pivot point.

Loss of speed leads to a widening of the drift angle as well as to a forwarding of the pivot point. It is by means of minimal changes in drift angle and position of pivot point that lateral resistance and rudder force preserve a competitive balance. As it is, the relationship between rudder force, drift angle, lateral resistance, and pivot point is intimately interwoven (fig. 122).

2. Steering Lever and Lateral Resistance Lever

Steering lever and lateral resistance lever remain constant when the ship is turning at a constant speed. Steering lever means the distance from rudder to pivot point; it can be rated as a first-class lever. The moment of the lateral resistance is the product of FR and lateral resistance lever.

The distance from the pivot point to R' is the lever of the lateral resistance (fig. 121); it can be rated as a second-class lever. The steering moment is the product of rudder force and steering lever.

Steering lever and lateral resistance lever are interdependent; conjointly, they are a double lever for the turn.

Under full ahead on the engine on full rudder, when the ship is momentarily at zero longitudinal speed, the pivot point will be at a distance from the bow of one beam (B). The steering lever will for this short moment be the ship's length minus the beam (L−B). When the ship is under speed, this initial steering lever will be reduced by $\frac{1}{4}$ to $\frac{3}{4}$ (L−B). The lateral resistance lever is $\frac{1}{2}$ (L−steering lever)

Steering lever = $\frac{3}{4}$ (L −B)

Lateral resistance lever = $\frac{1}{8}$ (L + 3B)

3. Turning Circle

The diameter of the full speed, full rudder, turning circle is directly proportional to the steering lever and inversely proportional to the lateral resistance lever. Expressed in ship lengths:

$$d = \frac{\frac{3}{4}\,(L-B)}{\frac{1}{8}\,(L+3B)} \times L, \text{ or } d = \frac{6\,(L-B)}{L+3B} \times L$$

The circumference of the turning circle is $C = \pi d$. The drift angle is the angle

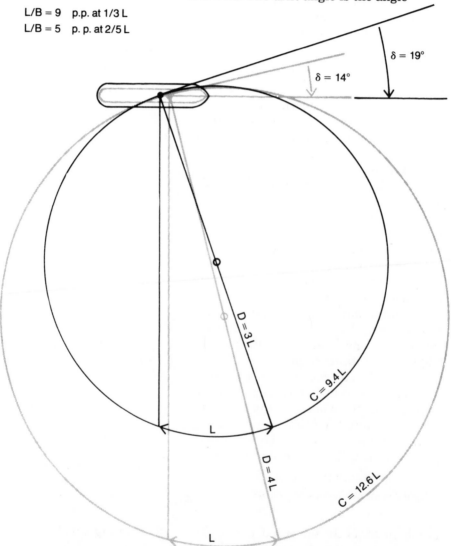

L/B = 9   p.p. at 1/3 L
L/B = 5   p. p. at 2/5 L

δ = 19°

δ = 14°

D = 3 L

C = 9.4 L

L

D = 4 L

C = 12.6 L

L

Fig. 123. Theoretical turning circles and drift angles (δ) for different L/B ratios.

between fore and aft line and the tangent to the turning circle at the pivot point. When we take for the drift angle $(\delta) = L/C \times 180°$, we find:

L/B	p.p.	d	C	δ
9	⅓ L	4 L	12.6 L	14°
8	21⁄32 L	3.8 L	12 L	15°
7	5⁄14 L	3.6 L	11.3 L	16°
6	⅜ L	3.3 L	10.5 L	17°
5	⅖ L	3 L	9.4 L	19°

The L/B ratio makes for the difference in diameter of the full speed turning circle of ships of about the same deadweight, trim, draft, and bottom clearance.

The diameter of the full speed turning circle of the first 90-degree turn is larger than the diameter of the ultimate complete turning circle. Two factors are responsible for the fact that the ship ends up the complete turn inside of the starting point. First, the initial effect of the rudder starts out with the pivot point farther forward. Consequently, the first stage of the turn, with the initial higher speed, is made under a larger steering lever, a greater AR and a smaller drift angle, resulting in a wider turn. Second, the original momentum carries the ship farther ahead and sweeps the ship farther away from the turn in the first stage of the turn. Loss of speed leads to loss of momentum in the later stage of the full turn.

4. Turning in Own Length

The turning couple can be made up by two tugs pushing with equal force in opposite directions at opposite ends of the ship. The pivot point is amidships; maximum underwater resistance is at the ends of the ship.

The continuation of the turn, after stopping the tugs, depends on the rotational momentum. The turn lasts longer when the mass is at the ends of the ship. Once the swing is on, it takes time to stop the turning motion with rudder and engine because of the short distance from rudder to pivot point (fig. 124, B).

Ships down by the head and relatively wide beam ships have their pivot point relatively close to amidships when turning under rudder; their handling characteristics are as follows:

A short steering lever, consequently slow steering response.

A strong lateral resistance force at the bow contributing to a small turning circle.

A large moment of rotational momentum of the foreship, together with a small steering lever, making it difficult to stop a swing.

A fast rate of turn.

5. Turning with Transverse Force on the Bow

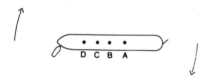

Fig. 124. Turning with the aid of a single tug.

A, the force exerted by the tug, is greater than the rudder/propulsion force; the pivot point is abaft midships (fig. 124).

Tankers in ballast, coming in to the monobuoy in a head wind (see figure 29) are better kept under control by rudder and engine than by a tug pushing forward. As the pivot point tends to come sternward under a forward push, the transverse wind-force is given too much leverage later on when rotational momentum has swung the bow through the wind, minimizing in this way the rudder leverage.

B, the force exerted by the tug, is equal to the rudder/propulsion force; the pivot point is amidships; the diameter of the turning circle is 1 L.

C, the force exerted by the tug, is less than the rudder/propulsion force; the pivot point is forward of amidships.

D, the force exerted by the tug, is zero; the underwater resistance constitutes the

lateral force. The pivot point will eventually settle at about ⅓ L from the bow. The
diameter of the full speed, full rudder
turning circle averages 3.5 L, depending
chiefly upon B/L ratio, trim, draft, and bottom clearance.

Fig. 125. Turning against the tug.

Ships trimmed by the stern and narrow
ships have good steering because of a long
steering lever. Under prolonged rudder to
one side, however, the strong lateral resistance abaft the pivot point prevents the
drift angle from widening up, resulting in
a wide turning circle.

E, the force exerted by the tug, is contrary to the rotational motion that we
want to set in by using propulsion force on
full rudder. The swing is against the tug
(fig. 125). When the propulsion force is
greater than the force exerted by the tug,
the ship will describe a wide turning circle, the diameter of which depends upon
the relative strength of tug and propulsion force. If the ship is prevented from
coming ahead, the longitudinal forces of
tug and propulsion force cancel out, and
only the transverse forces remain. The
transverse force of the tug is opposing the
turn, or the force exerted by the tug is
negative to the swing and causes the pivot
point to be far forward.

When we want to turn the ship into a
big sea or swell, we have to overcome a
similar negative lateral force at the bow
as far as rotational motion is concerned.
The transverse force of sea and swell at
the bow not only opposes the swing into
the direction of this force, but also brings
the pivot point forward, causing a slow
and wide turn against sea and swell.

When we apply counter rudder to stop
the ship from turning and to steady up,
the transverse rudder force has initially a
shorter steering lever than before the

swing set in because the FR forced the pivot point back. Under counter rudder (fig. 17) the FR acts as a negative rotational transverse force at the bow. As long as the FR acts in opposite rotational direction as the rudder force, the pivot point will be far forward, resulting in a slow and wide turn against the transverse force at the bow.

6. Turning with Bow Thruster

A bow thruster or a forward tug will turn the ship that is dead in the water, about a point, approximately a beam's distance from the stern (fig. 126). When, during the turning, we come ahead on the engine on full rudder, contrary to the swing, we have, initially, very little result in stopping the swing. The rudder force has little rotational effect because the point of impact is too close to the pivot point. After inertia has been overcome, the pivot point travels forward, providing more leverage to the transverse rudder force.

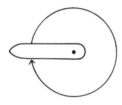

Fig. 126. Pivoting about the stern.

Applied in the opposite direction, rudder force and transverse force forward form a turning couple. Working in the same direction, rudder force and transverse force forward work as a team to give the ship lateral motion.

When we want to create lateral motion by using rudder and bow thruster, we must be careful not to overpower the bow thruster with the rudder force. Once a swing and forward motion develop from a powerful thrust on the rudder, the bow thruster works too close to the pivot point to have sufficient leverage to match the rudder force. On the other hand, if we have to apply stern power and we want to continue our lateral motion to port, we must be watchful to keep the bow thruster force in balance with the transverse thrust of the propeller. Once a swing develops from working the bow thruster on full power, it is the transverse thrust of the propeller that works too close to the pivot point, especially so when stern power has been applied a bit too long and stern motion has set in. In that case, a strong swing to port of the bow may even cant the stern to starboard against the transverse thrust of the propeller. In this way we can kill our lateral motion to port by an overdose of bow thruster force, as excessive motion of the bow to port has to be counteracted by working the bow thruster the other way. This is the situation as shown in figure 41, where the ship is not coming closer to the dock, in spite of desperate efforts.

The anchor on the bottom exerts a force in the opposite direction to the propulsion force (fig. 127). When the ship remains stopped in the water, with the engine working ahead, it means that the force exerted by the anchor equals the propulsion force.

Under rudder effect, the stern moves sideways, and the ship describes a circle, the diameter of which depends on the amount of chain that is lifted from the bottom. Much engine power may lift all the chain from the bottom; but when low engine power is used, there will be no strain on the the chain, and only a short scope of chain is moved around by the ship. Once a swing is on, the engine power is mainly translated into rudder force.

Participants in the shiphandling training course were interested in finding out if it was possible to turn a loaded 250,000-dwt tanker on the anchor. We tried it out with a model tanker of that size, and we found that very little strain was put on the chain with dead slow ahead on the engine and hard over rudder. Low engine

7. Turning on the Anchor (Loaded Ship)

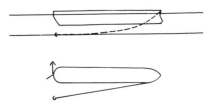

Fig. 127. Loaded VLCC turning on the anchor.

revolutions of the turbine result in very low engine power. The chain can easily stand the strain, provided we bring the ship very gently up into the chain. It is the shock load that breaks the chain, and not a constant strain, not even if the engine were to be working full ahead. However, the maneuver should not be attempted in current condition because of the very strong force of a current on the beam, with possible disastrous effect.

Since the ship swings on a very limited scope of chain, it is interesting to find out where the ship actually pivots. The pivot point must be far forward because it is the stern that moves around. As there is no strain on the chain, there is practically no force exerted by the anchor to push the pivot point back; with no speed through the water, there is no significant underwater resistance to make itself felt forward on the ship. Both factors plead for very limited engine power.

The propeller thrust is almost entirely spent on continuing the swing and overcoming lateral resistance. With a large moment of swing, the limited power is still very effective. As the fully laden ship has not too much above-water area, we can even swing the ship against a moderate beam wind (no current).

It is surprising to see how little strain there is on the chain. From the hawsepipe the chain drops almost vertically to the water, from where it starts to lead slightly aft. A short scope of chain would be enough, but it would absorb less of the initial forward motion of the ship. The weight of the chain and the longitudinal inertia of the ship absorb the part of the kinetic energy generated by the propulsion force which is not translated into transverse rudder force. In this case the longitudinal inertia of the big ship is an asset which we can use to advantage by applying limited engine power.

A tanker in light condition, set over the anchor chain, has difficulty in turning the stern into a wind on the beam (fig. 128). Minimum engine power causes very little strain on the chain and will keep the pivot point far forward, providing the wind-force on the beam with a long lever. The small rudder force, produced by low en-gine power, cannot overcome the wind-force in a strong beam wind (fig. 128, A). The farther the vessel is set over the chain the more difficult it is to set in the desired swing, as the transverse force ex-erted by the chain is negative to the swing and tends to keep the pivot point forward. By slowly increasing the engine revolu-tions, we not only increase the thrust on the rudder and our turning force, but also the tension in the chain.

The increased longitudinal pull of the chain forces the pivot point back, reducing the leverage of the wind-force. The lever of the rudder force also reduces as the pivot point comes back, but by increasing the thrust on the rudder we increase the turning moment (fig. 128, B).

In a strong beam wind we may apply full engine power to start the swing against the wind. Once the swing has set in, the pivot point moves forward again with an easing of the tension in the chain under the turn. When the stern moves up to windward, the angle between wind di-rection and ship's heading decreases, di-minishing the transverse wind-force. As the swing progresses we can gradually reduce the engine power.

8. Turning on the Anchor (Light Ship)

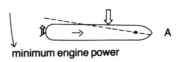

minimum engine power

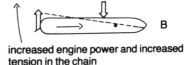

increased engine power and increased tension in the chain

Fig. 128. Light ship turning on the anchor.

Comparison Table

Dimensions, Diameter Turning Circles, Stopping Distance

KDWT	LBP feet (meters)	B feet (meters)	HP	Velocity in knots	Turning circle	Stopping distance
25	540 (164.6)	75 (22.9)	12,000	16	3.6 L	8 L
36	620 (189)	90 (27.4)	14,000	16	3.6 L	9 L
50	700 (213.4)	100 (30.5)	16,000	16	3.6 L	10 L
70	760 (231.6)	115 (35.1)	19,000	16	3.5 L	11 L
100	810 (246.9)	130 (39.6)	22,000	16	3.4 L	12 L
140	880 (268.2)	140 (42.7)	26,000	16	3.4 L	13 L
190	980 (298.7)	155 (47.2)	30,000	16	3.4 L	14 L
250	1080 (329.2)	170 (51.8)	35,000	16	3.4 L	15 L

Stopping distance means normal full astern. A crash stop or emergency may cut the stopping distance by about 25 percent.

References

Ardley, R. A. B. *Harbour Pilotage*. London: Faber & Faber, 1952.

Armstrong, M. C. *Practical Ship Handling*. Glasgow: Brown, Son and Ferguson, 1980.

Baer, W. *Assessment of Tug Performance*. London: International Tug Conference, 1969.

Bartlett-Prince, W. *Pilot Take Change*. Glasgow: Brown, Son and Ferguson, 1956.

Bowditch, Nathanial, original author. *American Practical Navigator: An Epitome of Navigation*. Washington, D.C.: U.S. Government Printing Office, 1977.

Célérier, Pierre. *La Manoeuvre des Navires*. Paris: Presses Universitaires de France, 1955.

Cockcroft, A. N. *Nicholls's Seamanship and Nautical Knowledge*. Glasgow: Brown, Son and Ferguson, 1979.

Cotter, C. H. *The Master and His Ship*. London: Maritime Press, 1962.

Crenshaw, R. S. *Naval Shiphandling*. Annapolis: Naval Institute Press, 1975.

Danton, G. L. *The Theory of Practice of Seamanship*. New York: St. Martin, 1965.

English, J. W. and B. N. Steel. "The Performance of Lateral Thrust for Ships as Affected by Forward Speed and Proximity of a Wall." London: N.P.L. Ship Division Report SH R 28/62, 1962.

Helmers, Kapt. W. "Messergebnisse von wichtigen Manoevriereigenschaften." *Hansa* (November-December 1961).

Layton, C. W. T. *Dictionary of Nautical Words and Terms*. Glasgow: Brown, Son and Ferguson, 1958.

Lorant, Michael. "Investigation into High Speed of Underwater Craft." *Nautical Magazine*, vol. 200: 5, 1968.

Nordstrom, H. F. *Screw Propeller Characteristics*. Stockholm: Publications of the Swedish State Shipbuilding Experimental Tank, 1948.

Pierens, C. "Draaicirkels." *De Zee*, nos. 4-5 (April-May 1970).

Plummer, C. J. *Ship Handling in Narrow Channels*. Cambridge, Md.: Cornell Maritime Press, 1966.

Sjostrom, Carl H. *Effect of Shallow Water on Speed and Trim*. New York: S.N.A.M.E., 1965.

Stunz, G.R. and R.J. Tayler. *Some Aspects of Bow Thruster Design.* New York: S.N.A.M.E., 1965.

Terrell, Mark. "Anchors—a New Approach." *Fairplay International Shipping Journal,* no. 4, 624, 1972.

Trott, B. "Waves, Flow and Drag." *Nautical Magazine,* vol 206: 6, 1971.

Willerton, P. F. *Basic Shiphandling for Masters, Mates and Pilots.* London: Stanford Maritime, 1980.

Woerdemann, F. *Dampfermanoever.* Berlin, Frankfurt/M: Mittler, 1958.

Zeevaartkundig Tijdschrift. De Zee. Raad voor de Scheepvaart (Shipping Council) reports on collisions in the Amsterdam North Sea canal: 1964, 4; 1965, 4; 1966, 6; 1970, 7.

Index

References to figures are printed in italics.

135

Index

HENRY H. HOOYER, a graduate of the Nautical College at Amsterdam, Netherlands (1947) began his seafaring career as a cadet on a passengership. He sailed on freighters and was employed for ten years by a large tanker company in various ranks. His first command was a coastal supply vessel which took him along the coast of West New Guinea and into the headhunting region. In 1960 Captain Hooyer became harbor master at West New Guinea and did piloting at Hollandia, Sorong, and Muturi Oil Terminal. When West New Guinea became part of Indonesia in 1962, he left that part of the world to become harbor pilot at San Nicolas, Aruba, Netherlands Antilles. In 1967, he accepted a two-year assignment as instructor at the newly opened Shiphandling Training Center at Grenoble, France, where a fleet of model tankers in the one to twenty-five scale is operated on an eight-acre lake. He then returned to real ships. He was a mooring master at Sidon, Lebanon; senior harbor pilot at Ras Tanura, Saudi Arabia; and marine advisor at Single Buoy Mooring Inc. at Monte Carlo, Monaco. Assignments took him to, among other places, Libya, Egypt, India, and the North Sea. He was back in Aruba in 1981 as docking master and training instructor for pilots, returning to Monaco at the termination of the three-year assignment. In 1993 Captain Hooyer was made a fellow of the Nautical Institute.

ISBN 0-87033-306-2

52400

9 780870 333064